AUG - - 2019

Making
Money Simple

Making
Money Simple

The Complete Guide to Getting Your Financial House in Order and Keeping It That Way Forever

Peter Lazaroff

WILEY

Library of Congress Cataloging-in-Publication Data is Available:

ISBN 978-1-119-53787-8 (Hardcover)
ISBN 978-1-119-53782-3 (ePDF)
ISBN 978-1-119-53785-4 (ePub)

Cover Design: Wiley
Cover Images: background © in-future/Getty Images, money house ©
ValentynVolkov/Getty Images

Printed in the United States of America.

V10008428_022719

Contents

Introduction

My first distinct memory of money was during a night out with my family at a local pizza shop. I don't remember how old I was, but I'd guess no older than six or seven. The restaurant had a jukebox and I asked my dad for money to pick out a song. Instead of handing over some change, my dad asked, "Is it worth your money?"

I told him no and he responded, "Then it's not worth mine."

The next time we went to that restaurant, I found myself eyeing the jukebox again. And again, I asked my dad for some money to pick songs on the jukebox. My dad asked the same question: "Is it worth your money?"

This time, thinking I was clever, I said yes. Then my dad said, "Great, then you can spend your own."

This lesson in the value of money is one of my most vivid memories as a child. My parents generally did the right thing with money: they didn't spend more than they earned and they were good savers. But beyond that, they didn't sit down and teach me about money. Money wasn't an off-limits topic, but it also wasn't a focal point of our routine family dinners. My perception is this isn't uncommon among most families.

So when do we get an opportunity to learn about money?

We don't learn about money basics in elementary school. We don't teach high school seniors how to budget or pay bills. Most college graduates don't take a course in personal finance or receive an unbiased education in the right way to invest money. It's even more unlikely they took a deep dive into financial planning topics like how to plan for retirement, buy a home, save for a child's education, or any other situations in life that require an understanding of how to manage money.

In school, you are given a lesson, then a test. In life, you are given a test and then you learn a lesson—and money lessons can be expensive.

I was fortunate in that I took an interest in basic personal finance as a teenager. It started when my grandmother gave me a share of Nike stock for my 12th birthday. I remember sitting in my parents' living room near the Christmas tree (I have a December birthday) and thinking this gift was boring relative to the video games I also received.

But then we started talking about the mechanics of investing and how the share of stock meant I had an ownership stake in one of my favorite brands. Maybe it was the fact that Nike seemed to be worth more every time I checked the newspaper or maybe it was the dividend checks I received for doing no work at all, but it didn't take long for me to be hooked on the idea of investing.

A few years after that birthday, my parents took me to the bookstore to buy an investment book geared toward young adults. The first one I picked out was Peter Lynch's *Learn to Earn: A Beginner's Guide to the Basics of Investing and Business*. This book is arguably the most influential book I've ever read. Not necessarily because it was the best book, but it was the source that turned an interest into an obsession.[1]

In high school, I asked my parents to subscribe to the *Wall Street Journal* so that I could read the Markets section. In college, I devoured books and periodicals on investing, personal finance, and economics. My parents were thrilled because I didn't like reading throughout most of my childhood. But reading about finance was different. Making good money decisions fascinated me. It was like solving a puzzle. There was a way to "win," which appealed to my competitive personality. And while I deeply regret not reading more of my assigned materials in high school, to this day I can't figure out why some of these financial issues weren't being taught in the classroom, too.

What I read in those investment books stuck with me, and even before I reached adulthood, I was laser focused on making the right decisions with my money. As a kid, I worked as a referee for youth basketball games in the winter. In the summer, I worked as a camp counselor on the weekdays and then a car wash and restaurant on the weekends. I contributed the money I made from these seasonal jobs to a Roth IRA even before I went off to college. That early start with finances and investing set me up for success year after year in my adult life.

I didn't start with a lot of money. I didn't use any complicated strategies in an effort to beat the market. From the ages of 13 to 18, I worked and earned a little cash. I read some basic information and consumed enough material to stay interested and engaged. And I invested in the stock market.

---

[1] You can find investment and personal finance book recommendations in the Conclusion.

There was no magic involved, no trademarked secrets. Starting early and keeping things simple laid the groundwork for my financial success in adulthood. Regardless of when you start, you can use this blueprint for success, too.

THE MOST POWERFUL TOOL IN YOUR FINANCIAL TOOLBOX

"I just want to make sure I'm doing the right thing."

That's what most people want when they start asking questions about their finances. Maybe you are just finishing college or graduate school. Maybe you just started earning enough to begin start saving more or aggressively paying down debt. Maybe you just had a child and need to understand how to manage your increased expenses (along with a whole new set of child-centric financial goals). Maybe you inherited money and want to ensure you make the most of it.

Regardless of your specific situation, we all need to understand our money and what to do with it. That's not easy to do on your own. The earlier I can reach a person in their life, the bigger the impact I can make on their financial success. That's not because I'm going to help them earn a few extra percent on their investments. It's because I'm going to leverage the power of compounding by putting systems and processes in place that encourage good financial behaviors.

Financial success isn't magic; it's engineering. And time is the most powerful tool in your financial toolbox. Time allows compound interest to grow wealth exponentially. Time allows basic investment theory to hold true. Time and thoughtful planning allow you to make your hard-earned dollars support the life you want to live.

For most of my career, I've been known as an investment expert. This reputation was built by helping countless individuals and institutions as a financial advisor by distilling complicated investment issues into understandable information. Along the way, I've also written monthly articles for the *Wall Street Journal* and *Forbes* while sharing my insights across a wide spectrum of national media outlets. Today I'm the Chief Investment Officer at Plancorp, which manages billions of dollars for clients across the country. I'm also the Chief Investment Officer of BrightPlan, a digital advisor designed to democratize fiduciary advice.

Despite those credentials, this isn't an investment book. Yes, investments are a very important part of a financial plan and we will talk about the fundamentals here. But it's so important to understand that fancy, convoluted investment strategies don't ultimately determine financial success. What this book will do is take you step by step through the process of getting your financial house in order and keeping it that way forever.

ENVISION WHAT YOU WANT, THEN CREATE A PLAN TO GET THERE

All too often, people make money decisions without the end goal in mind. They focus on the near term instead. What I recommend is starting with questions like these: What is your perfect money situation? How much would you need to be happy?

I'm not asking for a dollar amount. Picture your life with money never being a concern. For me, that means not worrying about whether each and every purchase is worth it. I order what I want at a restaurant. I take a vacation to the destination of my choice as time and logistics dictate. I live in the house that I want. I want to maintain my existing lifestyle and the comforts that I've worked hard for throughout my career. This is what the perfect money situation looks like to me.

What does financial success look like to you? We'll outline the steps you need to take in order to achieve your perfect money life.

IT'S NOT EASY, BUT IT DOESN'T HAVE TO BE HARD

There are very few things that people delay more than taking steps to improve their finances. It's cliché, but I frequently compare getting financially fit to getting physically fit. We all know we should eat healthily and exercise regularly, and yet most people don't abide by these simple rules. Perhaps the lack of immediate results is what discourages people from going to the gym five times a week or avoiding late-night snacks. For others, maybe it comes down to struggling to find the time or maintain the discipline required to live a healthy lifestyle.

Improvements to your health aren't achieved after a single 30-minute workout or a week of healthy eating. But the amazing thing about money is that you can permanently improve your finances with a single 30-minute activity such as automating your finances or completing one of the worksheets provided in this book (all worksheets can be downloaded at **peterlazaroff.com/worksheets**). It sounds easy enough, but there are some common obstacles people face when making these simple improvements in their life.

For starters, the number of choices and deciding where to start tends to paralyze people. For example, research shows that employee participation in 401(k) plans decreases when more investment options are available.[2] But this phenomenon isn't limited to finance alone. It's part of human nature.

One of my favorite examples of this comes from a study of shoppers sampling jams at an upscale food market. One day, shoppers saw a display table with 24 varieties of gourmet jam and received a $1 off coupon for sampling any jam. On another day, shoppers received the same coupon for $1 off any jam, but only six varieties of the jam were on display. When the time came to purchase, people who saw the smaller display were ten times likelier to buy jam than the people who saw the larger display.[3]

In personal finance, the number of choices and complexity of each underlying option makes it difficult to get started. The purpose of this book is to give you a clear starting point, focus only on the most important decisions to make, and create a saving system that quietly nudges your finances in the right direction without regular effort on your part.

A second problem people face with personal finance is a lack of clear-cut rules for financial success. Financial success, and the path to achieving it, is different for everyone. There isn't a perfect fix for this issue, but this book aims to provide tools that apply to everyone and form a framework for thinking about decisions that are more personal.

A third problem is that the human brain isn't hardwired to make optimal money decisions. Our cognitive and emotional biases create tremendous barriers to financial success. I've included lots of examples and discussions around these biases to help you become more aware of the mental errors we make, and I've also provided strategies to combat them.

Finally, and perhaps most importantly, people get discouraged by the speed of their progress. When you make good financial decisions, it takes time to see the impact. Much like physical exercise, you won't have a six-pack after a single trip to the gym. But unlike exercise, which requires constant action over a long period of time, improving a single area of your personal finances takes only 30 minutes and the benefits can last a lifetime. You just need to allow them time to work.

---

[2] Sheena S. Iyengar, Gur Huberman, and Gur Jiang, "How Much Choice Is Too Much? Contributions to 401(k) Retirement Plans," *Pension Design and Structure: New Lessons from Behavioral Finance,* Chapter 5, Oxford Scholarship Online, January 2005.

[3] Sheena S. Iyengar and Mark R. Lepper, "When Choice Is Demotivating: Can One Desire Too Much of a Good Thing?" *Journal of Personality and Social Psychology* 79, no. 6 (2000), 995–1006.

THE GUIDANCE YOU NEED FOR THE FINANCIAL SUCCESS YOU WANT

The financial industry doesn't always have your best interests at heart. You may be sold different products and solutions based on the person sitting across the table. More and more people are promising to act as fiduciaries—the fiduciary standard requires that an advisor put the client's interest first—but they aren't being policed the way they should be.[4] I've worked as a fiduciary my entire career. The information in this book is derived from the same advice I give to clients at Plancorp and BrightPlan. The tools and resources are the same ones my wife and I use. Now I want to teach you the things that matter most in driving your financial success.

Innovations in the world of finance will continue to shape the way we manage our financial lives, but good financial advice will never change. If you read this book from start to finish, you will have a game plan for setting and reaching your life goals with minimal ongoing effort. But before we do any of that, your journey starts with learning how to leverage the most powerful tool at your disposal: time.

---

[4]The fiduciary standard creates a legal obligation for financial advisors to put the interests of clients before their own. In addition, anyone selling investment products or providing investment advice to the public must disclose any conflicts of interest that might compromise that fiduciary duty. Every person working with an investment professional should get him or her to commit in writing to act as a fiduciary at all times.

CHAPTER ONE

The Power of Time and Compounding

The most powerful tool you have for reaching your goals is time.

Time mixed with the power of compounding is the most potent combination for wealth creation. Compound interest allows you to grow wealth faster by earning a return on your past returns. This isn't a linear relationship; it's exponential, and that power is the most underappreciated component of a financial plan. The human brain simply isn't good at visualizing exponential things, which may explain why it's so difficult to fully appreciate a plan that fully leverages the power of compounding.

Let's try to fix that.

Imagine you take a sheet of standard printer paper with a thickness of 0.1 mm. Fold it over once and it gets twice as thick. Fold it again and you've doubled the thickness of the paper again; two folds make the paper four times as thick. Fold it a third time and now the paper is eight times as thick. If you could fold that piece of paper 50 times, the paper would stretch 95 million miles or approximately the distance from Earth to the sun. At 100 folds, it matches the radius of the universe (see Figure 1.1).

Unfortunately, it isn't possible to fold a piece of paper more than eight times (try, I dare you). But the underlying math of repeatedly doubling the thickness of paper is exciting when we apply the same exponential growth to your savings.

FIGURE **1.1**   THE THICKNESS OF A FOLDED PIECE OF PAPER

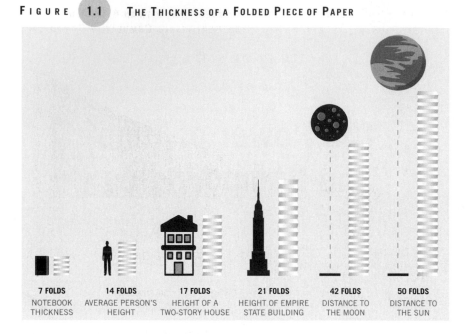

7 FOLDS	14 FOLDS	17 FOLDS	21 FOLDS	42 FOLDS	50 FOLDS
NOTEBOOK THICKNESS	AVERAGE PERSON'S HEIGHT	HEIGHT OF A TWO-STORY HOUSE	HEIGHT OF EMPIRE STATE BUILDING	DISTANCE TO THE MOON	DISTANCE TO THE SUN

THE POWER OF COMPOUND INTEREST

How many times can you double your money during your lifetime? That depends on your age and rate of return. With these inputs, we can use a rule of thumb known as "The Rule of 72." Simply assume a reasonable rate of return for planning purposes (between 7 percent and 9 percent over a multidecade time period) and divide 72 by that rate. This calculates the period of time it would take for your money to double.[1]

To make the math nice and even, let's say we earn an 8 percent return on your money. According to the Rule of 72, it takes nine years to double your money ($72 \div 8 = 9$). Ready for the compounding part? (See Figure 1.2.)

Let's start with $10,000 and continue to assume we earn a return of 8 percent. After nine years, the Rule of 72 tells us we will have $20,000. It should seem obvious that the $20,000 then takes another nine years to double, so we will have $40,000 after 18 years. As we will see in a moment, the earnings on interest becomes disproportionately larger than the earnings on the initial investment.

[1] The Rule of 72 is an approximation. The equation is $2 = 1 \times (1 + \text{Rate of Return})^Y$, where Y is the time to double.

FIGURE 1.2 GROWTH OF **$10,000** INVESTMENT WITH AN **8** PERCENT
RETURN: INITIAL INVESTMENT VERSUS CUMULATIVE COMPOUND
INTEREST

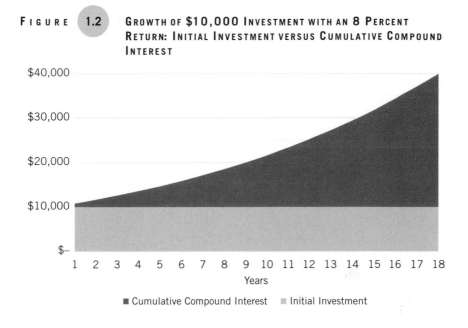

To see how good planning can maximize the benefit of compound interest, we can draw from Benjamin Franklin's financial plan. At his death, Franklin's will left 1,000 pounds sterling (then worth about $9,000) to his adopted home of Philadelphia and his native city, Boston.[2]

Franklin wanted trustees to loan the money to apprentices, much in the same way he received assistance early in his career. His will also stipulated that the interest collected from the loans should stay invested so it could compound over time. After 100 years, both cities could withdraw 75 percent of the funds to use for infrastructure projects that would improve the quality of life for those living in these cities like bridges, roads, water systems, and public buildings. Then in another 100 years, the cities could withdraw the remaining balance for additional infrastructure and city betterment projects.

Franklin estimated a 5 percent annual rate of returns from the loans. It turned out to be 4 percent. He was off by one percentage point, but remember that financial success depends less on marginally higher returns than it does on saving and time. This case serves as a perfect example of this phenomenon.

The cities made their first withdrawals in 1890. The fund grew from Franklin's initial contribution of $9,000 to $500,000 over a period of

[2]The Last Will and Testament of Benjamin Franklin, http://www.constitution.org/primary sources/lastwill.html.

100 years (that's about $13 million in today's dollars). When the cities could make their second withdrawal in 1990, they gained access to another $6.5 million (or $12 million in today's dollars). Franklin understood the power of compounding. He knew that good planning and time were the essential ingredients to having it work in your favor.

You probably won't get to work with a 100-year time horizon, but you will get several decades to allow your investments to earn compound returns if you start saving now. The way Franklin structured his will provides a great illustration of how thoughtful planning and time can best capture the power of compounding. The more time you have, the more your wealth benefits from this compounding effect. Once you create a well-thought-out financial plan that focuses on maximizing your wealth as a means to meet your goals, you can sit back and let time do its thing.

MAKE COMPOUND INTEREST WORK FOR YOU: SAVE EARLY AND SAVE OFTEN

The most important rule in planning for retirement is to save early and often. How early and how often? Start as soon as you begin earning an income and save some of every paycheck. If you haven't been saving, then the time to start is now. Saving early gives you what we've just seen is critical to leveraging the power of compounding: a long time horizon.

Compound interest is like rolling a snowball downhill. As it rolls along, it collects more snow with each rotation. The further it rolls, the more mass it can exponentially gain. That's exactly how Benjamin Franklin's initial $9,000 contribution turned into $500,000 over 100 years with a 4 percent rate of return. It's also why Warren Buffett says, "Life is like a snowball. The important thing is finding wet snow and a long hill." The wet snow is the interest you reinvest to pick up even more interest as you roll along. The long hill is the multiple decades you give yourself if you start saving early.

Figure 1.3 returns to our simple example of a $10,000 investment that earns 8 percent each year. Even though the interest rate remains unchanged at 8 percent, the amount of interest income increases every year. Just as a snowball accumulates more snow with each rotation as it increases in size, your investment generates a greater amount of earnings as the return is applied to a larger amount each year.

Over time, the interest earned surpasses that of the initial investment, which you can see in Figure 1.4. If you withdraw the interest earnings each year rather than reinvesting those earnings, then you receive $24,000 in interest payments over 30 years ($800 per year). However, reinvesting

F I G U R E   1.3   GROWTH OF **$10,000** INVESTMENT WITH AN **8** PERCENT RETURN: INCREASE IN INTEREST EARNINGS

Year	Value	Interest Earnings	Increase in Interest Earnings from Previous Year
1	$10,000	$800	—
2	$10,800	$864	$64
3	$11,664	$933	$69
4	$12,597	$1,007	$74
5	$13,605	$1,088	$81
6	$14,693	$1,175	$87

F I G U R E   1.4   GROWTH OF **$10,000** INVESTMENT WITH AN **8** PERCENT RETURN: CHANGES IN PROPORTIONS OF INITIAL INVESTMENT VERSUS EARNINGS OVER TIME

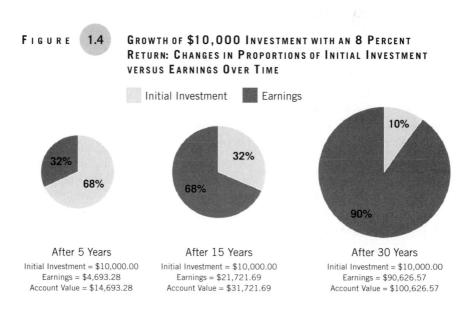

☐ Initial Investment   ■ Earnings

After 5 Years
Initial Investment = $10,000.00
Earnings = $4,693.28
Account Value = $14,693.28

After 15 Years
Initial Investment = $10,000.00
Earnings = $21,721.69
Account Value = $31,721.69

After 30 Years
Initial Investment = $10,000.00
Earnings = $90,626.57
Account Value = $100,626.57

the interest each year earns you an additional $66,626 in interest on top of the $24,000 earned by the initial investment. While this math is compelling on its own, saving early creates an even more impressive impact.

Let's imagine two recent college graduates named Michelle and Matt, who each earn an 8 percent rate of return on their investments. Michelle starts investing today by making a $250 contribution each month to her retirement account. After ten years of these monthly investments, Michelle

FIGURE **1.5**   THE IMPACT OF SAVING EARLY IN LIFE

Michelle	versus	Matt
$250	Monthly Contributions Years 1–10	$0
$0	Monthly Contributions Years 11–40	$250
10 Years	Number of Contributions Years	30 Years
$30,000	Total Contributions	$90,000
8%	Hypothetical Growth Rate	8%
$509,605	Value After 40-Year Period	**$375,074**

needs the $250 to cover additional expenses related to relocating for a new job. She doesn't make any further contributions to the account and doesn't touch the balance until she retires 30 years later.

Matt, on the other hand, is still in the college mindset and figures there is plenty of time to save for retirement later. Ten years from now, he begins investing $250 every month until he retires 30 years later. Whose nest egg is bigger at retirement? Let's take a look.

As you can see in Figure 1.5, Michelle comes out ahead despite contributing less money to her account for fewer years than Matt. The secret behind Michelle's success? Starting early, which gives her a longer time horizon than Matt. As your time horizon increases, so does the effect of compounding. Even though Michelle made a smaller total contribution, her investment had more time to benefit from the effects of compounding.

Now, you can see why the most important rule of retirement savings is save early. For what it's worth, if Michelle or Matt had found a way to save $250 a month from the time they graduated college at age 22 to the day they retired at age 67, they would have retired with $1,318,635. In other words, saving less than $10 a day can add up to over $1 million in wealth. Can you find an extra $10 a day to contribute to your investment account?

It's easy to procrastinate with savings, particularly for long-term goals such as retirement, but understanding the power of compounding should convince you to do otherwise. Of course, we shouldn't forget that the exponential power of compounding can work against you, too.

THE DARK SIDE OF COMPOUNDING

The impact of inflation also compounds over time, but this is *not* good news. Inflation works against you by decreasing the buying power of your hard-earned savings. For example, a dollar bill acquired at the founding of the Federal Reserve in December 1913 and tucked under the mattress for safekeeping would buy a mere four cents of what it snared back then. Inflation has historically averaged about 3 percent. According to the Rule of 72, that means your purchasing power gets cut in half every 24 years.

Investment costs and taxes create a similar drag on your rate of return. Let's continue with the previous example in which you save $250 a month into an investment account that earns 8 percent a year from age 22 to age 67. Without costs and taxes, you would retire with $1,318,635. Because investing is not a costless activity, let's assume you pay 1.5 percent for investment-related fees. These fees come directly out of your 8 percent return and reduce your ending balance to $807,125.

Taxes also reduce returns if you aren't using a tax-deferred account like an IRA or an employer-sponsored retirement plan. The impact of taxes will vary by your state of residence, income level, and mix of investment accounts. Given all the variables, let's simply assume that you pay taxes equal to 6 percent of your investment balance each year. Continuing with our example from before, the ending balance after costs and taxes comes to $713,230. In other words, the negative impact of compounding from investment fees and taxes wiped out more than half of your investment account.[3]

Another area that compounding can work against you is when you take on debt. Unfortunately, many people need to take on debt at some point in their lives. Most people could not afford a home without a mortgage. Many others couldn't pay for higher education without student loans. These are both examples of good debt because they can positively contribute to your overall net worth. Unlike a car that depreciates in value the moment your drive it off the dealer's lot, a home's price generally appreciates at a rate similar to inflation. As for education, student loans are an investment in your ability to earn a higher income.

Credit card debt, on the other hand, is bad debt because it's typically the result of unnecessary consumption or poor planning—and, more importantly, comes with high interest rates and low minimum payments.

---

[3] The tax rate used in this example is a round number since everyone has different tax circumstances. The gains realized from selling assets you hold less than 12 months are subject to the short-term capital gains tax rate, which is equal to your highest marginal ordinary income tax bracket. The gains realized from selling assets you hold 12 months or longer are subject to the long-term capital gains rate, which is 15 percent for married couples filing taxes jointly earning between $78,751 and $488,850. Married couples filing taxes jointly earning $488,851 or more will pay a 20 percent capital gains tax. Unless you live in a state that has no income taxes, you will also owe state income tax on your gains. All of the income levels and tax rates in this footnote are as of 2019. Visit www.irs.gov for current tax brackets.

That combination of factors plus compound interest makes the cost of using credit cards enormous. Imagine buying a new TV for $2,500 using a credit card with a 16 percent annual percentage rate (APR) and making minimum payments of $50 until the balance is paid off. In this scenario, compounding creates $3,994 in interest costs over the nearly 22 years it takes to pay off the original $2,500 purchase.

SMALL DECISIONS AND GOOD HABITS LEAD TO BIG RESULTS

It's simple to achieve financial success if you can make decisions that take advantage of the power of compounding over time. Whether you're saving early and often, systematically adding to your investment portfolio, or staying the course in times of uncertainty, time has the power to turn small habits into incredible results.

The problem is there are lots of decisions to make. Should you invest or pay down debt? Where should you keep cash savings? What types of investment accounts should you use first? Should you rent or buy a home? What percentage of your income should you save? The decisions you make today will have compounded effects decades later—but before you can start making good choices, you first must take time to figure out what you're trying to get out of life.

CHAPTER TWO

Where Do You Want to Go?

Financial success doesn't just happen; it's incremental. This can be a challenge for many people because you don't see immediate results. Similarly, it's hard to make progress without knowing where you're trying to go. That means you must start with the end in mind. Figure out where you want to finish, and then work backward to set up everything you need to get there.

If you're not sure where to start, picture your future self in 30 years. Set down this book right now, close your eyes, and focus hard on envisioning yourself decades from now. What do you look like? How are you dressed? Where are you? What are you doing? Who else is there?

Now think about when your kids are headed to college. What does that look like? What do you want to do with your time once you have an empty nest? Will you move? Take up a new hobby or even try a "second act" career? You have a blank canvas here, which can be overwhelming. I'll share my own vision if you need a little inspiration to start dreaming about what this situation looks like in your own ideal world:

> *I'm accompanying my oldest son to college. The school has a Division I sports program, which excites me because I went to a Division III school and now I have a better reason to watch college football and basketball. I'm trying to play the cool dad since my son seems a touch embarrassed by my presence. I'm dressed like the other parents. I take my son up to his dorm room and think to myself, "Was I really able to live in this small a space?" I'm not worried about how I will afford all of this because I've been making monthly contributions to his 529 plan since the year he was born. My plan has always*

been to cover roughly 70 percent of his college costs with a 529 plan and the remainder from my current income, but my early start at saving for his education resulted in me being able to fund 85 percent of his tuition through the 529 plan.

Now picture yourself the night before your final day of your career. Tomorrow, you'll start your retirement:

I'm sitting down to dinner with my wife at our home on a Thursday night. Tomorrow night we will go out to dinner to celebrate. My children don't live in town, but we are flying them in to join us. I'm thinking about playing golf on Saturday. I'm thinking about the trip my wife and I have planned. My hair has grayed and thinned. I've added a few pounds, but I'm not over-weight. My wife has aged, too (sorry, honey). I'm still in my work clothes, but they aren't trendy by any stretch of the imagination. After dinner, I head into my living room to turn on the Cardinals game and pull out my reading device. I have a glass of really nice bourbon—not because I'm about to retire, but because at this ripe age of 70, I buy and drink nice bourbon. It's part of the lifestyle I've worked hard for and systematically saved for to ensure that I can continue living my life the way I want to live.

Now, it's your turn. Take a moment to think about where you see yourself in 20 years, 30 years, and beyond. What do the major turning points of your life look like? What kind of lifestyle do you want to have as you move through the seasons of your life? What activities do you want to enjoy and what kind of skills or knowledge do you want to gain through the years? What does your home look like? Do you travel?

Allow yourself to really dream. There are no right or wrong answers. It's just about coming up with a vision that you can start working toward. Once you spend some time thinking about what your future looks like, write it down. That makes it more real and keeps you focused on taking the right actions to turn your dreams of the future into reality. The **Goal Planning Worksheet** shown in Figure 2.1 is designed exactly for this exercise. (You can download full copies of all worksheets referenced in this book at **peterlazaroff.com/worksheets**.)

All too often, people make money decisions without considering the impact on their future. In fact, research shows that our brains think of saving as a choice between spending money on ourselves today versus giving it to a complete stranger.[1] Economists refer to this as intertemporal choice, or choices made about the timing of consumption.

[1] Hal E. Hershfield, G. Elliott Wimmer, and Brian Knutson, "Saving for the Future Self: Neural Measures of Future Self-Continuity Predict Temporal Discounting," *Social Cognitive and Affective Neuroscience* (March 2009), 85–92.

FIGURE 2.1   GOAL PLANNING WORKSHEET

Priority	Short-Term Goals (5 Years or Fewer)	Completion Date	Expected Cost
			$
			$
			$
			$
			$
			$
			$
			$
			$
			$
Total Expected Cost of Short-Term Goals			$
Required Monthly Savings to Reach All Goals in 5 Years			$

Here's one way to think about this: if given the choice of going to a great dinner today versus a year from now, most people will choose the great dinner today. Or suppose I offered you the choice of a $25 Starbucks gift card today or three months from now. Unless you intend to quit drinking coffee in the next three months, free coffee today is unlikely to be more valuable today than in three months (time value of money aside). But when asked to predict their happiness, people expect to experience more happiness from receiving the gift card today than three months in the future.[2] Perhaps this outcome would be different if people stopped for a moment to picture themselves in the future, sipping on a latte while chatting with a friend on a cold morning.

This is why the exercise of dreaming is so important. It may seem silly, but don't skip over this step in formulating your financial plan. Several studies have shown imagining the future leads to increased patience when choosing between your current and future selves. One team of researchers even took this concept a step further by having people interact with realistic renderings of their future selves within a virtual environment.[3]

[2] Karim S. Kassam, Daniel T. Gilbert, Andrew Boston, and Timothy D. Wilson, "Future Anhedonia and Time Discounting," *Journal of Experimental Social Psychology* (November 2008), 1533–1537.

[3] Hal E. Hershfield, Daniel G. Goldstein, William F. Sharpe, Jesse Fox, Leo Yeykelis, Laura L. Carstensen, and Jeremy N. Bailenson, "Increasing Saving Behavior through Age-Progressed Renderings of the Future Self," *Journal of Marketing Research* (November 2011), S23–S37.

In a series of experiments, participants looked into a virtual reality mirror that captured their movements but reflected back age-progressed versions of themselves. One of the studies asked participants how they would allocate an unexpected windfall of $1,000. The participants were given the choice of buying something nice for someone special, investing in a retirement fund, planning a fun and extravagant occasion, or putting it into a checking account. The group that saw an aged version of themselves allocated more than twice as much money to the retirement account than participants who only saw their current selves in the mirror. In all iterations of their research, researchers found that interacting with photorealistic age-progressed renderings of themselves caused people to allocate more resources to the future.

By really thinking hard about the big life moments in the decades that lay ahead, you can start to define the end destination. Once you know where you're trying to go, you can create a plan to get you there. This isn't a one-time exercise, though; you will need to revisit your plan at least annually because life will bring changes along the way that require adjustments.

An analogy I use for the many adjustments required in a financial plan is the way pilots develop flight plans from New York to San Francisco. First, they look at factors such as air traffic and weather to plot their most likely course. Mid-flight, pilots must adjust their flight plan for any number of reasons, but they will still end up in San Francisco. A good financial plan does the same. It maps out a plan of action to get you from beginning to end using the available information about the future. The world is constantly changing, as is your own life, so your plan will change, too. But if we don't determine the end destination in advance and how to make the necessary adjustments along the way, you might end up in Toronto instead of San Francisco.

THE IMPORTANCE OF WRITING OUT YOUR GOALS

Now that you've had an opportunity to envision your future, it's time to put the pen to paper. Writing down a goal with an estimated date and expected cost dramatically increases your likelihood for success. It also allows you to clarify the things that are most important to you.

To get started, visit **peterlazaroff.com/worksheets** and download the **Goal Planning Worksheet**. The first step is writing down short-term goals (five years or fewer), the date of desired completion, and the expected cost. If you add up the expected cost of all your goals, you can determine how much you need to save on a monthly basis to make this happen over the next five years.

To give you an idea of how this works, Figure 2.2 depicts short-term goals from the **Goals Planning Worksheet** that a newlywed couple, Andrew and Casey, filled out for me in 2017. If you are just getting started or the dollar amounts seem discouraging, remember that financial goals come in all shapes and sizes. Andrew and Casey are fortunate to have good jobs and very little debt, but the system I'm teaching you works for everyone.

There is no such thing as a final draft of your financial plan. Short-term goals often change from year to year, whereas intermediate- and long-term goals tend to be more static. Much like the example of a pilot creating a flight plan, you should revisit your goals on a regular basis to accommodate life's inevitable changes.

For example, the retirement goal in Figure 2.2 changed in 2018 when Casey got access to a 403(b) through her new employer. Once they begin having children, I suspect they will add new goals such as saving for college or finishing their basement. They are also likely to increase the size of their emergency fund goal to accommodate the higher living expenses that successful professionals inevitably take on.

FIGURE 2.2 SAMPLE SHORT-TERM GOALS, COMPLETION DATES, AND EXPECTED COSTS

Priority	Short-Term Goals (5 Years or Fewer)	Completion Date	Expected Cost
1	Max out IRAs and Andrew's 401(k) every year	$29,500/year	$147,500
2	Build emergency fund	July 2022	$30,000
3	Pay off student loans	December 2019	$15,500
4	Save for "big" 5-year anniversary vacation	July 2015	$12,000
5	Buy Casey a new car	October 2020	$35,000
			$
			$
			$
			$
			$
Total Expected Cost of Short-Term Goals			$240,000
Required Monthly Savings to Reach All Goals in 5 Years			$4,000

Once you record your short-term goals, complete the same exercise for intermediate-term goals that will take 5 to 15 years to accomplish. The importance of this exercise is to understand the things that are important to you in life and, from a financial perspective, how much you need to save in the future. Some examples of intermediate goals I see people set include buying a car, having children, buying a rental property or vacation home, saving for college, taking a once-in-a-lifetime vacation, saving more for retirement, paying down a specific debt, and so on.

It's common for intermediate-term goals to have higher expected costs, which means your monthly savings will need to be greater than the level needed to meet your short-term goals. Even if you don't have enough income to save for your intermediate-term goals today, you might invest in a mix of stocks and bonds so that your money can compound at a higher rate of return to close the savings gap. You may also close any savings gap through a rising income or gradual increases to your savings rate.

Finally, be bold and come up with some long-term goals that are at least 15 years away. It may be difficult to assign an expected cost to your long-term goals, but that's okay. Your long-term goals speak volumes about your financial values, so just thinking about it is more important than perfectly estimating costs. Typical long-term goals are headlined by retirement or financial independence, but also tend to include items like paying for a child's education, enjoying extensive travel, buying a dream home, owning a vacation property, giving to charity, and leaving a legacy.

PRIORITIZE YOUR GOALS (AND START WITH THESE CRITICAL TWO)

Now that everything is listed out, it's time to rank your goals. This will be important as you start designing your financial plan, because understanding your priorities can help simplify the more complex decisions. If you do this exercise with a significant other, then it also facilitates meaningful conversations about your future and builds a mutual understanding about what's most important to both of you.

The **Goal Planning Worksheet** includes a column to assign a priority rank to each goal and the remainder of this chapter is dedicated to determining how to rank various goals. The top two priorities for your short-term goals should be retirement and emergency fund. Retirement as a top priority for short-term goals may surprise you because it will undoubtedly be part of your long-term goals, but you need to make retirement contributions a high priority in the near term. (Remember that whole discussion on giving compound interest the time it needs to do its thing?) Equally important is establishing an emergency fund to avoid situations that can derail your progress by impeding your ability to take advantage of compounding growth.

Saving for Retirement

The top priority on everyone's list should be saving for retirement. Your short-term and intermediate-term goal worksheets should list specific retirement savings amounts, while your long-term goal worksheet should identify the estimated date you'd like to retire and the amount of money you want to spend each year. But where should you direct investment dollars? Is it more important to max out a 401(k) before an IRA? At what point should you use a taxable account for retirement savings? How does debt play into these decisions?

This is one of those truly personal finance moments because everyone has different circumstances. Making the optimal decision requires knowing:

1. Your current tax bracket as well as your expected bracket at retirement
2. Your current income and expected income in retirement income
3. The amount you must invest
4. The likelihood you will tap retirement assets before retiring
5. Your retirement plan options and costs

To simplify the many variables that go into the decision-making process, here's the general order in which I recommend saving for retirement.

1. **Invest enough in your employer-sponsored retirement plan to earn a match.**

    It's hard to find a guaranteed 100 percent return on your investment, but an employer match does just that. If your employer offers a match on some portion of your 401(k) contributions, invest at least that much. Otherwise, you leave free money on the table. Other examples of an employer-sponsored retirement plans are 403(b) and 457 plans.

    For example, if your employer has a 3 percent match and your salary is $100,000 a year, you'll need to contribute at least $3,000 of your own money to be entitled to your employer's full matching contribution. Once you invest at least enough in your employer plan to receive the match, then move on to the next account.

2. Invest in a Roth IRA or deductible Traditional IRA.

For people with multiple decades until retirement, the flexibility and tax advantages make the Roth IRA the next best place to direct your retirement savings. Unfortunately, there are income restrictions for Roth contributions based on your modified adjusted gross income (MAGI). If your income is too high to invest in a Roth IRA, then the next best option is a deductible Traditional IRA.[4]

Figure 2.3 lists the income limitations for Roth contributions and deductible Traditional IRA contributions. If your income is too high to qualify for a Roth IRA or a deductible Traditional IRA, you can still contribute to a nondeductible IRA and enjoy tax-deferred growth, but that option is a little further down the list.

Both Roth and Traditional IRAs allow your money to grow tax-free, but the difference (see Figure 2.4) is the timing of tax payments. A Roth IRA is funded with after-tax dollars, meaning your contributions don't receive an income tax deduction. But your withdrawals from a Roth IRA are tax free. A deductible Traditional IRA, on the other hand, is funded with pre-tax dollars and you pay ordinary income tax on the withdrawals you make in retirement.

3. Invest the maximum allowable amount in your employer-sponsored retirement plan.

Once your first two buckets are full, you can work to max out your contributions to an employer-sponsored retirement plan, such as a 401(k). Your plan may allow you to make contributions to a traditional 401(k) or a Roth 401(k).

If you expect to be in a higher tax bracket during retirement than you're in today, the Roth 401(k) is the superior option. If you expect to be in a lower tax bracket during retirement than you are today, the Traditional 401(k) is the option for you. If you aren't comfortable projecting whether your taxes will be higher or lower at retirement, consider making contributions to both the Traditional and Roth options. This strategy is known as tax diversification.

---

[4]My preference for funding a deductible Traditional IRA before maxing out an employer-sponsored retirement plan is driven by my past experiences working with people who have employer plans with high fees and poor investment options. However, one downside of building a Traditional IRA balance before maxing out an employer-sponsored retirement plan is that it decreases the opportunities for you to do a Roth conversion described later in this section.

FIGURE   2.3   ROTH AND TRADITIONAL IRAS: INCOME LIMITS FOR TAX YEAR
2019

ROTH IRA		
Filing Status	**Contribution is limited if Modified Adjusted Gross Income is between:**	**No contribution if Modified Adjusted Gross Income is over:**
Single/Head of Household	$122,000 and $136,999	$137,000
Married filing jointly	$193,000 and $202,999	$203,000
Married filing separately	$0 and $10,000	$10,000
DEDUCTIBLE TRADITIONAL IRA FOR INDIVIDUALS COVERED BY AN EMPLOYER PLAN*		
Filing Status	**Deduction is limited if Modified Adjusted Gross Income is between:**	**No deduction if Modified Adjusted Gross Income is over:**
Single/Head of Household	$64,000 and $73,999	$74,000
Married filing jointly**	$103,000 and $122,999	$123,000
Married filing separately	$0 and $9,999	$10,000

*Individuals or married couples without an employer-sponsored plan such as a 401(k),
403(b), or 457 can make contributions to a deductible Traditional IRA, regardless of income.
**If only one spouse is covered by an employer plan, the deduction is limited if your Modified
Adjusted Gross Income is $193,000 to $202,999, and the deduction is eliminated if your
Modified Adjusted Gross Income exceeds $203,000.

Employees of nonprofit entities with access to a 403(b) should aim
to max out that vehicle at this stage. The same goes for government
employees with access to a 457 plan. Smaller employers sometimes
provide a Simple IRA or a simplified employee pension (SEP) IRA
option, both of which fall into this retirement savings prioritization
category, too.

4. Invest in a nondeductible Traditional IRA.

Nondeductible Traditional IRA contributions receive no tax ben-
efit, but they do enjoy the benefit of tax-deferred compound growth.
Because tax-deferred growth is the only tax benefit, a nondeductible
IRA is most useful to investors under the age of 40.

For some investors, contributing to Traditional nondeductible
IRAs and converting the balances at a later date to a Roth IRA may

FIGURE 2.4   KEY DIFFERENCES OF ROTH AND TRADITIONAL IRAS

	ROTH IRA	TRADITIONAL IRA
Best Suited For	An individual who expects to be in a higher tax bracket when he/she starts taking withdrawals	An individual who expects to be in the same or lower tax bracket when he/she starts taking withdrawals
Maximum Contribution (2019)	$6,000 ($7,000 for age 50 and older)	$6,000 ($7,000 for age 50 and older)
Funded Using	After-tax dollars	Pre- or after-tax dollars
Contributions Grow	Tax-free	Tax-deferred
Withdrawals	Tax-free withdrawals after five years and age 59½ Tax-free distributions allowed for first-time homebuyer expenses up to $10,000	Penalty-free after age 59½ All earnings taxed as ordinary income
Mandatory Distributions	None	After age 70½

prove advantageous, but that should be considered only when you have the guidance of a financial advisor.[5]

5. **Invest in a taxable account.**

If you've reached this point, congratulations! You're doing a nice job of saving for your retirement. While you've exhausted the best tax-advantaged options, you can always save in a taxable account. The key here is to be very aware of the tax efficiency of the investments you select.

Setting Up Your Emergency Fund

The next priority for your short-term goals should be an emergency fund. Many people don't have an emergency fund, which may be the result of the human tendency to believe bad things only happen to others.[6] A fully

---

[5]When you convert an IRA into a Roth IRA, you must pay ordinary income taxes on any appreciation and earned income experienced in any of your IRA accounts, not just the account being converted. The decision to convert a Traditional IRA to a Roth IRA requires an analysis of the immediate tax impact, your time horizon, your future tax bracket, and the desired beneficiary of the assets.

[6]This is referred to as optimism bias.

funded emergency fund is also difficult to build quickly, which may deter some people if they are impatient. Others dislike building cash reserves rather than investing for retirement or paying off debt.

Just because most people don't have an emergency fund doesn't mean you should go without one. Your emergency fund can help cover the cost of life's unexpected surprises such as medical bills, car repairs, job loss, and so on. People without this cash reserve are faced with tough decisions when one of life's unfortunate events pops up. Do you turn to credit card debt that charges a high interest rate? Do you have to take out an additional loan on your home? Do you dip into your 401(k)? If you dip into your investment portfolio during tough economic times, that can mean selling assets from your nest egg when the market is down or, alternatively, spending cash that could otherwise buy assets in your portfolio on the cheap. Any of these actions will set you back in growing your net worth and hinder your ability to reach your goals.

For this reason, setting up your emergency fund is something to work toward ASAP. An emergency fund should contain six to 12 months' worth of living expenses. Living expenses are those that you would continue having if you were to lose your job such as rent or mortgage, utilities, groceries, gas, insurance, and so on. Chances are that your actual monthly expenses, which I refer to as lifestyle expenses, are higher than your barebones living expenses. Within that range, the specific size of your emergency fund should correspond with your level of job security and the potential volatility of your income. For example, doctors and tenured professors have incomes that are more predictable and typically don't need as big of an emergency fund. On the other hand, someone whose income tends to fluctuate with the economy, such as a freelancer, start-up employee, or construction worker, may want to maintain a bigger emergency fund.

Setting aside six to 12 months' worth of living expenses requires a lot of cash, but don't let that prevent you from getting started. An emergency fund is rarely built overnight. If you start from scratch, the best way to build yours is to contribute a very manageable sum to a designated savings account every pay period—and make it an automated piece of your financial plan.

If you get paid on the 15th and 30th of the month, set up automatic contributions from your primary checking to a dedicated emergency fund account to occur on those dates each month. Start small to make sure you can still live comfortably with your remaining income. After a few months, make a modest increase to your emergency fund contribution. For example, if you decide to transfer $100 of each paycheck into your emergency fund, then you may increase your contribution to $150 after six months. After another six months, you could increase your contribution again to $200.

The best place to keep an emergency fund is in a money market fund or online bank account that is separate from your primary bank. Using an account outside of your primary checking bank makes it easier to resist the urge to dip into those funds for nonemergency purposes. Money market funds and online banks tend to pay higher interest rates than checking accounts at traditional brick-and-mortar banks. There will always be variation in who is paying the highest interest rate, but I've never found it worthwhile to chase the highest interest rates and earn a few extra fractions of a percent. When you're getting started, pick the option that has an interface you feel most comfortable using.

WHERE DOES PAYING DOWN DEBT FIT INTO YOUR FINANCIAL PRIORITIES?

Retirement savings and an emergency fund belong at the top of everyone's goals. You won't meet either of these goals overnight—and that's okay—but you need to consistently contribute to these goals to leverage the power of compounding. You want to make decisions that maximize your net worth, which in turn leads to financial freedom and security. But that raises an important question: how do you make the choice between investing versus paying down debt when deciding how to allocate your savings?

Everyone has different circumstances, but there are some common variables that can inform your decision:

- Expected return on investments
- Interest rates on debts
- Tax benefits associated with your debt
- Tax benefits associated with investing
- Matching contributions
- Private mortgage insurance
- Loan forgiveness clauses
- Variability of your income
- Number of years to retirement

Evaluating these variables can help you arrive at the best solution from a purely mathematical perspective. But this decision is based as much on your personality as it is the math. Some people prefer paying down debt to capture a lower, but knowable, return. Others prefer investing to capture higher, but less predictable, returns.

There is no one-size-fits-all advice, but we can use some general guidelines to think through the problem. Here's how I believe it makes the most sense to prioritize investing and debt repayment decisions as you are ranking your goals.

1. **Make contributions to your employer-sponsored retirement plan up to the level at which your employer matches.**

   If your employer will match the first 3 percent of your contribution, then take advantage of that free money and contribute 3 percent to your retirement plan.

2. **Pay down debt with a high interest rate (at least 8 percent) that is not tax deductible.**

   Credit card debt and personal loans are good examples. These debts tend to have high interest rates and the interest payments are not tax deductible. (Interest on student loans and a mortgage are often tax deductible.)

3. **Make the maximum contributions to tax-advantaged investment accounts like employer-sponsored retirement plan and IRAs.**

   As of 2019, the maximum contributions for someone under 50 years old is $19,000 to a 401(k) and $6,000 to an IRA. If you are over 50 years old, the maximum contribution is $25,000 to a 401(k) and $7,000 to an IRA.[7]

4. **Pay down your mortgage if it requires you to pay private mortgage insurance (PMI).**

   You need to pay PMI if you put less than 20 percent down on your home purchase. PMI payments make mortgage debt more expensive, so you should focus on paying down the mortgage until you have home equity of at least 20 percent and, thus, can eliminate the need for PMI.

5. **Pay down debt with a high interest rate (at least 8 percent) that is tax deductible.**

   Student loans are a good example of debt with a high interest rate, but the interest on student loans is tax deductible, which lowers the effective interest rate that you pay.

---

[7] Visit www.irs.gov for the most current information on retirement account contribution limits.

6. **Contribute to investment accounts with no tax benefits where you expect to earn returns greater than the interest rate on remaining outstanding debt.**

   This means investing in a diversified portfolio of stocks and bonds in an investment account such as an individual account, joint account, or trust (if you have a trust in place). All capital gains, dividend income, and interest income is fully taxable.

7. **Pay down debt with interest rates that are less than 8 percent.**

   Your last priority should be prepaying low-cost debt because these offer the lowest return to your overall net worth. These days, a mortgage or home equity loan are good examples of low-cost debt that could also give you a tax deduction. Auto loans typically fall into this lower-cost debt category, but they don't have the benefit of a tax deduction.

Your unique circumstances and money personality may dictate a reranking of some categories. Assuming you can meet your regular minimum debt service payments, maxing out tax-deferred accounts can have a strong mathematical advantage depending on your tax bracket and time horizon. On the other hand, a desire to be debt-free may emotionally outweigh the math. Oftentimes, directing cash across multiple categories rather than just one at a time makes sense. In these situations, it's important to understand your emotions and perception of financial freedom. If you need help, using an objective third party that acts as a fiduciary at all times can help you work through these decisions and set up an intentional, systematic plan that meets your life goals.

So far, we've only talked about goals tied to maximizing your net worth such as saving for retirement, setting up an emergency fund, and paying down debt. But life shouldn't be only about maximizing your net worth. You have to make room for the fun stuff, too.

GETTING THE MOST OUT OF YOUR SPENDING

Now that you're equipped with some general rules for prioritizing financial goals, we need to rank goals that are tied to consumption. After all, the quality of the journey is just as important as the destination. While your retirement savings and emergency fund are the nonnegotiable top priorities, there isn't a "right" way to rank your goals. There will always be a mathematically optimal way to prioritize your goals, but consumption-based goals are often tied to emotions that can't be captured in such an analysis.

When it comes to prioritizing your consumption-based goals, the aim should be to prioritize those that will make you the happiest by favoring experiences over material goods and prioritizing purchases that create time.

Favor Experiences Over Stuff

Consider the last several big-ticket material items you purchased. You probably got a lot of pleasure out of those items initially, but that happiness wore off as the novelty faded. There's nothing wrong with purchasing material items, but research suggests that experiential purchases like a vacation or an elaborate date night bring more happiness, which makes sense when you consider the lasting memories an experience can create.[8]

For example, I took a ski trip with friends in February 2009, which was near the nadir of the financial crisis. For weeks I considered not going because it seemed like a poor use of money during a severe recession, but my wife convinced me that staying home would be a huge mistake. She was right. That trip turned out to be one of my most memorable experiences with that group of people. I don't remember how much the trip cost, but I wouldn't exchange those memories for the money spent or anything I could have earned by investing those dollars instead.

Experiences become part of our identity by making us feel more connected to friends and family. On my deathbed, I won't remember the personal electronics I've purchased over the years. I will remember my ski trip as well as the many other trips, concerts, and sporting events I've spent with family and friends. My wife calls me cheap—I prefer frugal—but she will also tell you that my wallet is wide open when it comes to experiences from vacations and playoff baseball to live performances and special occasion dinners. These experiences provide lasting happiness by allowing me opportunities to deepen connections and relationships with others.

The other great thing about experiences is that you get to enjoy them in advance as well as when they're actually happening. In fact, the period leading up to an experience can be as fulfilling as the experience itself. Think about the last time you took a vacation. In the weeks or months leading up to the trip, you likely looked at pictures of your destination, talked about activities you plan to do, and bragged to your co-workers about the upcoming time off. You can also extract happiness in advance

[8] Leaf Van Boven and Thomas Gilovich, "To Do or to Have? That Is the Question," *Journal of Personality and Social Psychology* 85, no. 6 (2003): 1193–1202.
    Thomas DeLeire and Ariel Kalil, "Does Consumption Buy Happiness? Evidence from the United States," *International Review of Economics* 57, no. 2 (2010): 163–176.

of lower-cost experiences, like a date night, by thinking about how great it will be to relax with your significant other, how funny a movie might be, or how tasty a restaurant will be.

In my experience, people are too quick to deem an experiential purchase as too expensive. As you rank your goals, keep in mind that experiences are more likely to provide lasting happiness than almost any other purchase you save toward.

Prioritize Purchases That Create Time

Expenditures that eliminate the worst minutes of your day can provide a big boost to your happiness. For example, one of the best lifestyle expansions my wife and I made was hiring a home cleaning service. Neither of us likes to clean the house—my wife swears that I don't know how to pick up, but I'd argue I'm just meticulous in my method.

We resisted this added expense for a long time, but it's now one of the last things we'd cut in a pinch because there's real value in the time it creates for us to spend together. A cleaning service saves us about six hours per month, which we can use to do other things like exercising or family activities.

While it's easy to spend money to gain efficiencies, how you choose to use that found time matters. For example, I bought a second computer to improve my efficiency in between meetings or while traveling for work, but now I work more hours at home than I did before, which can affect my family's and my happiness. Consumption-based goals that save you time have the ability to increase your happiness, but they shouldn't be prioritized if you don't intend to use that time for something that will make you happier.

So far, we've spent a lot of time talking about where you want to go and dreaming about that future. It's the best place to start planning your journey to financial success.

Next stop? We need to look at where you are today. This will help identify which of your goals are obtainable in the short term. And for those that aren't obtainable right away, we'll start listing out the steps to help you reach them over time.

CHAPTER THREE

Where Are You Today?

T he previous chapters are important for laying the groundwork, but now you can get into the serious planning that will help set you up for financial success. You know where you want to go, but before you can start heading there, you need to understand where you are today. To do so, you'll need a **Net Worth Worksheet** and a **Cash Flow Worksheet**, both of which you can download from **peterlazaroff.com/worksheets**.

The **Net Worth Worksheet**, as seen in Figure 3.1, provides a snapshot of your overall financial health at a specific point in time.

Complete your **Net Worth Worksheet** by listing all your assets and liabilities in their respective categories. Once you've written down this financial information, you'll use these numbers to calculate your net worth. That represents where you are today. Why does this matter? Before making any personal finance decisions from here on out, you'll want to ask yourself two questions to help you choose your next course of action:

1. How does this affect my net worth?
2. How does this impact my ability to reach my goals?

The first question measures financial success in the traditional, mathematical sense. In most cases, making good financial decisions should lead to an increase in your net worth. Using your **Net Worth Worksheet** can be a useful tool when evaluating a major purchase such as taking an unplanned trip with friends or buying a new car. Spending money is not a bad thing. The key is to make intentional choices

FIGURE 3.1   SAMPLE NET WORTH WORKSHEET

NET WORTH: ASSETS

Taxable Accounts	You	Spouse	Joint	Total
Checking	$	$	$	$
Savings	$	$	$	$
Money Markets	$	$	$	$
Investments	$	$	$	$
Stock Options (Vested)	$	$	$	$
Other	$	$	$	$

Retirement Accounts	You	Spouse	Joint	Total
Traditional IRAs	$	$	$	$
Roth IRAs	$	$	$	$
401(k), 403(b), 457 Plans	$	$	$	$
Other	$	$	$	$

Personal Property	You	Spouse	Joint	Total
Real Estate	$	$	$	$
Cars	$	$	$	$
Business	$	$	$	$
Other	$	$	$	$
TOTAL ASSETS	$	$	$	$

NET WORTH: DEBT

Personal Property	You	Spouse	Joint	Total
Mortgage	$	$	$	$
Home Equity Loan	$	$	$	$
Car Loan	$	$	$	$
Credit Card Debt	$	$	$	$
Student Loans	$	$	$	$
Other	$	$	$	$
TOTAL DEBT	$	$	$	$

TOTAL ASSETS $	− TOTAL DEBT $	= TOTAL NET WORTH $

with your saving and spending so that you get the most value out of your money.

For example, an unplanned trip with friends may not be in your budget and will certainly reduce your net worth. But if you place a high value on travel and spending time with friends, then the hit to your net worth is well worth it. Plus, we know that experiences tend to generate longer-lasting happiness.

Examining a car purchase, however, is a bit trickier. Buying a car will always ding your net worth, but it's probably a necessary expense. It may even be a goal you meticulously plan and save for. But how might spending more on a nicer car affect your other goals? Framing decisions in the context of your goals can help you make better decisions and minimize regret. To better answer that question, you must complete the **Cash Flow Worksheet,** since that drives how much you can contribute to your goals.

UNDERSTANDING YOUR CASH FLOW

The **Cash Flow Worksheet** in Figure 3.2 requires you to list all your income sources and regular expenses so that you can determine how much cash flow you have available on a monthly basis to direct toward your goals.

Most people have a good grasp of their earnings and fixed expenses, but everyone has some variability in cash flow that can slip through the cracks. On the earnings side, some people receive bonuses or commissions that can get missed in a monthly constitution of cash flows. On the expense side, seasonal and one-time expenses (holiday gifts, summer vacations, auto repairs, home maintenance, and so on) are normal for just about everyone. My advice is to figure out what your spending was last calendar year and divide that total number by 12. Do the same for income. If you have multiple years of spending data, take the average annual expenditures and divide by 12.

Tracking your spending doesn't necessarily require hoarding receipts or endless spreadsheets. You can look at credit card or bank statements to calculate how much you spend. If you use a credit card for most expenses, simply go online and print off the annual statement for all of your cards, total the amounts, and divide by 12 to come up with an average of your monthly credit card expenditures. As an added bonus, most credit cards have annual reports that categorize your spending for you. Another option is reviewing your primary checking account to see exactly how much money flows in and out on a monthly basis.

The easiest way to track spending, however, is using a financial account aggregator. These tools make it much easier to manage your cash flow on an ongoing basis. Here's what to do:

1. Sign up for a financial account aggregator. I personally use Mint and BrightPlan, but there are many options that are easy to use.
2. Enter your bank accounts, credit cards, and investment accounts.
3. Sit back and be amazed at how easy it is to track your expenses when a system does it for you automatically.

FIGURE **3.2**   SAMPLE CASH FLOW WORKSHEET

INCOME: MONTHLY AMOUNT

Salary (Net: After Taxes and Benefits)	$
Spouse's Salary (Net: After Taxes and Benefits)	$
Interest/Investment Income	$
Other Income (Specify)	$
Other Income (Specify)	$
Total Monthly Income Amount	$

EXPENSES: MONTHLY AMOUNT

Mortgage or Rent	$
Other Real Estate Payments (Taxes, Assessment, etc.)	$
Loan Payments	$
Student Loan	$
Credit Card Payment	$
Utilities	$
Tuition	$
Child Care	$
Food	$
Subscriptions	$
Personal Care (Haircuts, Gym Membership, etc.)	$
Entertainment	$
Other Expenses (Specify)	$
Other Expenses (Specify)	$
Other Expenses (Specify)	$
Other Expenses (Specify)	$
Total Monthly Expenses Amount	$

INCOME $	– EXPENSES $	= TOTAL MONTHLY CASH FLOW $

Having an active Mint or BrightPlan account for a few months should provide enough data to determine your typical monthly spending rate. The longer you use these tools, the more accurate your spending estimate becomes and the easier it is to successfully plan for your financial goals. For example, planning for the retirement goal of "maintaining your current lifestyle without running out of money" is almost impossible unless you have a handle on what your current lifestyle costs.

Once you determine your monthly income and spending, you can see how much cash flow is left over for saving toward your goals. In other words, this is the point in the process where you can see if the goals you listed are attainable based on where you stand financially right now. Let's pull out your **Goal Planning Worksheet.**

Starting with short-term goals, add up the expected costs and divide by 60. This number is the amount you need to set aside per month to meet all your short-term goals over the next five years. Now compare this amount to the excess monthly cash flow on the **Cash Flow Worksheet**. If there is enough cash flow to meet these short-term goals, terrific! It may be time to start looking toward applying some excess monthly cash flow toward your intermediate-term goals.

If you don't have enough cash flow to meet your short-term goals, then priority ranking comes into play. Again, contributing to your retirement accounts and creating an emergency fund need to be the top two priorities no matter where you are in life. You don't need to max out every retirement account or build an emergency fund overnight, but you need to make meaningful contributions to give yourself the best chance of meeting your long-term goals.

After those top two priority items, does anything seem more important than the rest? Would you be equally happy if some of these goals came at a lower expected cost? Feel free to re-rank priorities, change estimated costs, or modify completion dates based on where you are today. That's the purpose of this exercise.

A common problem at this point of the process is discovering there is less monthly cash flow available on your **Cash Flow Worksheet** than what is required to reach your goals. If you're in this position, it's time to take a hard look at your current spending habits.

SPENDING TOO MUCH? HERE'S WHAT TO DO

The idea of cutting expenses is often talked about like a tragic event, but that isn't a productive way to frame the act of saving money. Saving isn't about making sacrifices; it's about keeping your priorities and getting more of what you really want.

There are many ways to make small contributions to your savings that involve delaying gratification or examining the importance of your everyday expenditures. Rather than the typical "cut out your Starbucks" advice, the first step is to skip all impulse purchases. When you go to any store, make a list of what you need to purchase. Don't purchase *anything* else.

If you feel like there is something else you need once you're at the store, ask if you need the item in the next week. If not, skip the purchase.

Now that you track your expenditures with a tool like Mint or Bright-Plan, you can try another trick to get your lifestyle expenses more in line with the things you enjoy most. Look at your recent spending and sort each expenditure into one of three categories: best value, good value, or low value. If you share expenses with a significant other, do this exercise separately and then compare notes. There will undoubtedly be other items you each ranked differently, but that's okay. Nobody is right or wrong here. Are there any items you both place a high value on? Those costs don't necessarily need to be cut right now. Instead, focus on the expenditures you both put in the low value category. These expenses should be eliminated immediately to free up a little cash each month to dedicate toward the things you really value in life.

SIMPLE CHANGES FOR BIG SAVINGS

Cutting expenses that offer little to no value is a painless way to boost savings with relative ease. Finding big savings, though, requires a little more work. Here are some areas that can make a big impact.

Buy term life insurance instead of permanent (whole life) insurance. If other people depend on your income, then you likely need or already have life insurance. Not only is term insurance significantly less expensive than permanent insurance, most people are better off with term insurance. Insurance salespeople earn a bigger commission for selling permanent insurance since it's more expensive, so you may face a sales pitch that makes a compelling case for a product you don't need. For now, know that term is likely your best bet (for exceptions and more information on life insurance, see Chapter 11).

Increase deductibles on your auto insurance. One way to lower your auto insurance bill is raising the deductible, which is the amount you pay out of pocket before the insurance benefits kick in. The higher your deductible, the less the insurance charges you for coverage. If you have an emergency fund that can cover the higher out of pocket expenses in the event of an accident, then this form of self-insuring is a no-brainer. If you don't have an emergency fund yet, then this strategy doesn't make sense.

Increase deductibles on your home insurance. Your home is likely one of the biggest (if not the biggest) assets on your personal balance sheet. No one purchases home insurance because it's fun. You need it because if that asset burns down, the financial impact of not having insurance would be devasting. Much like with auto insurance, you can save a significant amount of money by increasing your deductibles, but this only makes sense if you can afford to take on the additional liability in the case of an unforeseen event.

Trade in your travel rewards credit card for one that earns at least 2 percent cash back. People, including me, love miles and points, but a cash-back credit card might be more useful if you are spending too much to meet your goals. In my experience, most people aren't savvy enough with their spending and redemption strategies to make points more valuable than a simple cash-back reward. If your primary goal is to boost savings, cash-back credit cards offer an immediate return in value and flexibility that travel reward cards cannot match.

Refinance your loans. Refinancing debt to a lower interest rate can save you thousands of dollars on a mortgage, student loan, or other large debts. If you decide to refinance your loans, it is important to make sure the monthly cost savings will offset the loan origination cost and the additional interest expense that comes from resetting the term of your loan.

Buy cars less frequently. The average length of car ownership is 6.6 years.[1] That means the average person will buy nine or ten cars from the time they graduate college until the time they reach age 85. Driving your car for eight years means buying two fewer cars between the ages of 22 and 85. Compounding the cost savings from buying fewer cars over multiple decades would result in significant bump to your net worth. The cost savings can be highly impactful even if you do this with only a couple of cars, particularly in the first half of your career as you gain more time for the savings to compound.

Change your cable or streaming service plans. My family recently canceled our cable service. Netflix and Amazon Prime Video were already accounting for most of our TV use. The only thing keeping me connected to my cable company in the past was live and local sports channels, but now those are available on streaming services, too. We gain additional savings whenever we cancel a streaming service for a few months because we are too busy or we are actively watching a series on another platform. Cutting the cord saves us roughly $100 a month, which is outstanding, especially considering we didn't give anything up in the process.

---

[1] Jack Walsworth, "Average Age of Vehicles on Road Hits 11.6 Years," *Automotive News,* November 22, 2016.

IT'S TIME TO START YOUR JOURNEY

Now that we've identified where you are trying to go and where you stand today, we can begin putting systems in place to make the journey. The journey may be a long one—several decades for most people—so we are going to focus on habits that allow for incremental progress to turn into exponential results. All these steps can be accomplished on your own using the worksheets provided or with the help of a trusted financial planner who puts your interests first. If you begin feeling overwhelmed and want help, know that we'll talk more in Chapter 12 about how to find the right advisor to create a comprehensive financial plan for you.

CHAPTER FOUR

Creating a System for Financial Success

Did you ever have to read *The Odyssey* in high school?

Homer's epic told the story of Odysseus's journey home to Ithaca, which included a part in which Odysseus and his friends had to sail past the island of Sirens. The Sirens sang a song no sailor could resist, but if they steered their ship toward the island, they wrecked their vessels upon the rocks. Knowing this beforehand, Odysseus devised a plan to enjoy the Siren song while safely continuing toward his intended destination.

Odysseus instructed his crew to fill their ears with wax and sail past the Sirens no matter what. Odysseus then had the crew tie him to the ship's mast so he could listen to the Siren song without being tempted to steer toward the island. The plan worked beautifully. Odysseus was able to hear the Siren song without wrecking his ship. Even though he begged to be freed the entire time, the process he committed to in advance safeguarded him from foolish decision making.

In the present day, you face countless temptations in everyday life that can distract you from your stated goals when making financial decisions. Messages to consume never stop. Advertisers literally follow you around the Internet. Stores meticulously place and price merchandise to encourage impulse purchases. Social media make you hyperaware of all the stuff your friends and family members are buying. Meanwhile, it's never been easier to spend money thanks to one-click ordering, mobile payments, in-app purchases, and the increasing use of credit cards over hard cash.

As an investor, you face an even more complicated set of temptations. Wall Street spends billions of dollars convincing you to take action when you shouldn't. Financial media doesn't help, either. They cover markets as if investing is a daily activity and create a sense of urgency that doesn't exist if you develop and follow a thoughtful plan to stay on course. Repeat after me: Wall Street and the financial media are not on your team. The deviations these parties encourage from our intended course can lead to a financial mess.

Resisting modern-day Siren songs requires a system for saving that limits bad behaviors today and helps you make good financial choices for your future. In economics, this is called precommitment. It establishes processes that encourage good behaviors and help fight the temptation to deviate from a plan. On top of a good system, you may choose to leverage a human or digital advisor to play the role of Odysseus's crew, which means they need to have their ears plugged with wax (figuratively, anyway). They also need to remain objective, unbiased, and themselves undeterred by the noise of markets and media so they can succeed in their role. They should help you stay tied to your financial plan to ensure you sail safely past temptations and onward to your goal.

Whether you use an advisor or not, the systems described in this chapter will help you stay on course during your financial journey and enjoy life the way that Odysseus enjoyed the siren song (without actually tying yourself to a pole).

CREATE A BUDGET THAT ACTUALLY WORKS

Most people find it difficult to stick to a budget because the process is time-consuming and restrictive. Traditional budgeting forces you to make every decision as if you live in a spreadsheet. But guess what? You don't live in a spreadsheet!

Rather than focus on expenses, try prioritizing savings through a process I refer to as reverse budgeting. Reverse budgeting simply figures out how much you need to save, makes those savings automatic, and then allows you to spend the remaining money as you please. If you spend your budgeted amount on restaurants, but something very important comes up unexpectedly that requires dining out, you can shift spending elsewhere to fall in line with your priorities and values.

Reverse budgeting focuses on saving and paying yourself first. Because you can't spend what you don't have, increasing the amount you save naturally reduces the amount you spend, but it also forces you to prioritize your expenditures. This is important because most people find that gradually saving more allows them to cut spending that doesn't really fit with their values.

Best of all, reverse budgeting requires very little maintenance. A traditional budget requires weekly or monthly tracking of financial transactions. Once you set up a reverse budget, you can automate the entire thing. The lack of an ongoing time commitment makes it much more likely you will stick to a reverse budget. Here's how to set one up.

Step 1: Add Up the Amount Per Month That You Need to Save for Your Short-Term Goals

Pull out the **Goal Planning Worksheet** to determine how much you need to save on a monthly basis to reach your short-term goals. Next, rank the goals according to your priorities. This lets you know where to begin directing your monthly savings. Figure 4.1 shows how to do this using our example from Chapter 2 of Andrew's and Casey's short-term goals in 2017. To calculate their required monthly savings to reverse budget, we simply total their expected costs and divide by 60.

Now refer to the **Cash Flow Worksheet.** If there is enough money to cover the required monthly savings, then begin directing some cash toward your intermediate-term goals. If you can't meet the monthly savings required for your short-term goals, then try to escalate your savings over time (see the third step). You may also need to adjust your goals or consider the strategies discussed in the previous chapter for freeing up extra cash.

Step 2: Set Up a Monthly Automatic Withdrawal from Your Checking Account to a Separate Savings Account for Each Goal

Open online savings or brokerage accounts for each short-term goal. Using accounts that are separate from your primary checking account creates a barrier to impulsive spending by making the money more difficult to access. Opening multiple online accounts makes it easier to track progress toward each goal. For example, I keep specific accounts open titled Retirement, Emergency Fund, College, Vacation, and Car. Each month, I contribute specific amounts to each goal through an automated transfer.

FIGURE **4.1**   SAMPLE SHORT-TERM GOALS, COMPLETION DATES, AND
EXPECTED COSTS

Priority	Short-Term Goals (5 Years or Fewer)	Completion Date	Expected Cost
1	Max out IRAs and Andrew's 401(k) every year	$29,500/year	$ 147,500
2	Build emergency fund	July 2022	$ 30,000
3	Pay off student loans	December 2019	$ 15,500
4	Save for "big" 5-year anniversary vacation	July 2015	$ 12,000
5	Buy Casey a new car	October 2020	$ 35,000
			$
			$
			$
			$
			$
Total Expected Cost of Short-Term Goals			$ 240,000
Required Monthly Savings to Reach All Goals in 5 Years			$ 4,000

After opening your online savings accounts, set up automatic monthly withdrawals from your checking account in the amount reverse budgeted in the first step. Once you've automated the savings that will keep you on track for reaching your goals, you can spend the leftover money in your checking account as you see fit.

Step 3: Escalate Your Automatic Savings Over Time

Escalating automatic savings is a great tool for those who can't save the required monthly amount to meet their short-term goals. For example, Andrew's and Casey's short-term goals in Figure 4.1 required them to save 16 percent of their income—a very reasonable savings rate—but they hadn't been saving much at the time. That made finding $4,000 per month from their lifestyle a daunting challenge, but automation made it easier. Andrew and Casey started by contributing $2,000 per month to their various savings accounts. Every six months, their savings were set to automatically increase by $500. By the beginning of 2019, they were saving the $4,000 they had initially targeted, but decided to leave the automatic increases in place so that they could start saving toward intermediate-term goals.

Similarly, my wife and I could only afford to save $100 a month for our newborn son's college education in 2013. That wasn't going to be enough

F I G U R E **4.2**   H O W T O A U T O M A T E Y O U R I N C O M E , E X P E N S E S , A N D I N V E S T M E N T S

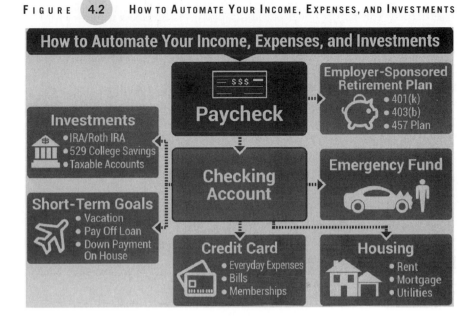

to reach our education funding goal, so every January, our monthly contribution for college savings automatically increases by $100. That means we saved $200 per month in 2014, $300 per month in 2015, $400 per month in 2016, and so on.

HOW TO AUTOMATE INCOME, EXPENSES, AND INVESTMENTS

Automation helps you achieve specific goals by systematically creating positive long-term habits. The benefits of automation align with the human tendency to embrace habits. In fact, more than 40 percent of the actions people perform each day are driven by habit rather than actual decisions.[1] Habits are a consequence of our brain's constant search for ways to conserve energy. Habits free up our mental capacity from thinking about basic behaviors such as walking or chewing our food so that we can devote mental energy to inventing spears, irrigation systems, and (eventually) the steam engine and computers.

[1] Bas Verplanken and Wendy Wood, "Interventions to Break and Create Consumer Habits," *Journal of Public Policy and Marketing* 25, no. 1 (2006): 90–103.

David T. Neal, Wendy Wood, and Jeffrey M. Quinn, "Habits—A Repeat Performance," *Current Directions in Psychological Science* 15, no. 4 (2006): 198–202.

Unfortunately, our brains don't differentiate between good habits and bad habits. And habits never really disappear. This makes it harder for me to avoid the cookies in the office lunchroom or mindlessly eating in front of the TV. Not only are humans creatures of habit, we also don't like change. Change requires more mental effort, which our brains are hardwired to avoid. Routines become automatic, but change jolts us into consciousness, sometimes in uncomfortable ways. Our preference to avoid change can be leveraged by automating good habits.

As Charles Duhigg wrote in *The Power of Habit:* "Willpower isn't just a skill. It's a muscle, like the muscles in your arms or legs, and it gets tired as it works harder, so there's less power left over for other things." It is important to visualize the future and keep our goals in mind when making financial decisions, but that requires a lot of willpower. However, the habit of contributing to a savings account every week requires very little mental energy, particularly given how easy it is to automate those good practices.

By putting your personal finances on autopilot, you take advantage of the human tendency to embrace habit. Plus, it's easier to do today than ever before.

Step 1: Open the Appropriate Accounts for Your Automated System

The first step of building an automated process is opening the right accounts. That starts with your primary checking account. Consider this to be like Grand Central Station for your money. Cash will constantly be coming and going on a predetermined schedule. To prevent the automation system from biting you, there needs to be a cash cushion in your checking account to protect against overdrafts.

The cushion doesn't need to be very big, and it shouldn't be considered a substitute for your emergency fund. Most people find that 25 to 50 percent of one month's expenses is sufficient. If you have less predictable income and expenses, then a full month or two of expenses is more prudent. Your cash buffer should act as a level to mentally associate with a balance of $0. For example, if your cash buffer is $5,000, then a balance of $5,000 should register as $0 to you. If you dip below that amount, you might consider exercising additional care with your expenses and payments.

After creating a cash cushion in your primary checking account, you should open online savings accounts that are tied to specific goals. Having an account for each goal allows you to tailor a strategy to the objectives and constraints of each goal. For example, savings going toward funding a newborn child's education can tolerate more risk and, thus, might benefit from being invested in the stock market. Alternatively, an emergency fund needs to be in cash. A dream vacation might fall somewhere in the middle.

The other accounts to use in the automation process are credit cards that earn rewards or cash back on your everyday spending. Credit cards are not for everyone, but responsible and strategic use of credit cards can provide your finances with an additional boost from automation.

Step 2: Pay Yourself First

Now that you have the appropriate accounts open, you can begin building the automation process by paying yourself first. Start by automatically directing funds toward the short-term goals in your reverse budget on the days your paycheck hits your primary checking account. Remember that retirement savings and an emergency fund must be the top two priorities of your short-term goals. Even if you have high interest consumer debt or student loans to pay down, you need to be contributing something toward retirement and an emergency fund.

Step 3: Set Up Payments for Your Bills and Expenses

Next, focus on your bills. Nearly all bills can be paid automatically. Credit cards, mortgage, rent, utilities, tuition costs, memberships, subscriptions, and more—automate them all to ensure you avoid late penalties. You should also use cash-back credit cards for any bills that don't assess additional fees for credit card payments.

Step 4: Automate Your Contributions to Your Investment Accounts

Arguably the most important step is automating your investments. Automatically investing at predetermined times protects you from making common market timing mistakes and allows you to diversify your purchase price over time. This process, known as dollar cost averaging, is discussed more in Chapter 8.

The easiest place to automate investments is within an employer-sponsored retirement plan such as 401(k), 403(b), or 457 plans. Assuming you have a good employer-sponsored retirement plan, this should be where most of your retirement dollars should flow until you've reached the maximum contribution. In Chapter 2, we discussed how to prioritize your retirement savings if you need a reference for automating your investments.

Step 5: Increase Your Automated Savings Over Time

The final piece of automating your finances is finding a way to automatically increase your savings over time. Many online investment platforms allow you to increase recurring contributions on an annual basis. The same goes for many online banks. If this feature is not available, I'd recommend creating a recurring calendar event for January 1 each year with specific instructions of how much you will commit to increasing your savings.

The primary benefit of automatic escalation is that it prevents lifestyle creep by directing earnings and raises to savings before you're tempted to spend it (or before you get used to having it in your account in the first place).

DEALING WITH LIFESTYLE CREEP

If you place your hand in a bowl of lukewarm water and start heating it, you're unlikely to notice the rising temperature. Your hand adapts to the gradual change. Eventually, the water will get to a point at which it's so hot it could burn you and you *will* notice, even if it doesn't instantly register. Remove your hand from the bowl of hot water and dunk it into a bowl of ice water, however, and you'll feel the temperature difference immediately—and it isn't going to feel good. Lifestyle creep happens to us in much the same way.

Most people get some kind of raise each year. Without a plan to save that raise, it's very easy to use it up by adding a few luxuries to your regular spending. It starts with little things: adding premium cable channels, buying more expensive bottles of wine, making more frequent phone upgrades, giving nicer gifts for birthdays, adding impulse items to your cart on Amazon, purchasing better seats at an event, staying in nicer hotels, paying for slightly nicer airline seating—the list of potential lifestyle upgrades goes on and on.

Each of those things individually doesn't seem harmful, especially as you earn more and can truly afford a few luxuries. But little things have a way of adding up. Before you know it, you adapt without even noticing. Lifestyle creep happens when your spending rises with your income and you adjust to a more expensive way of living. Once you get used to one or any of these upgrades, eliminating them is like dunking your warm hand into ice water. It becomes *very* hard to do.

Some inflation in your lifestyle isn't a bad thing, but you don't want the subtle upticks in your expenses to reach a point at which it makes reaching your goals more difficult. Research from the Federal Reserve

Bank of New York shows that most of your inflation-adjusted wage growth (aka, pay raises) will occur in your early working years before leveling off in your mid-career and peaking in your 50s.[2] Similarly, a study from the Labor Department shows that the greatest inflation-adjusted income growth comes in your 20s, but grows at a declining pace in your 30s and 40s.[3] That suggests it's crucial to have a system in place that keeps lifestyle creep under control when you receive raises earlier in your career. Creating a reverse budget and automating your finances help prevent the type of lifestyle expansion that is detrimental to your financial goals.

GET YOUR FINANCIAL HOUSE IN ORDER AND KEEP IT THAT WAY FOREVER USING AUTOMATION AND TECHNOLOGY

Creating a system for financial success is all about making intentional, systematic choices with your money. A good system will direct dollars to the things that matter most and keep you on track for reaching your end goals. A systematic process can also reduce or eliminate our human tendencies that lead to poor consumption choices as well as subpar saving and investment decisions. But the system should also make it all automatic.

In the past decade, we've seen a boom in financial technology that makes implementing such a system much easier. It wasn't all that long ago that managing your money required meticulous tracking of income and expenditures, diligent record keeping, and constant check writing to pay bills or contribute to investment accounts. That's all changed with the proliferation of digital tools that make tracking finances, setting goals, and investing simpler than ever before.

With a good savings system in place, we now turn our focus to investing. Successful investing allows you to maximize the impact of the good savings habits you've implemented in this chapter by offering a higher compound rate of return.

[2]Fatih Guvenen, Fatih Karahan, Serdar Ozkan, and Jae Song, "What Do Data on Millions of U.S. Workers Reveal About Life-Cycle Earnings Risk?" Federal Reserve Bank of New York, Staff Report No. 710, February 2015.
[3]Bureau of Labor Statistics, "Number of Jobs Held, Labor Market Experience, and Earnings Growth Among Americans at 50: Results from a Longitudinal Survey," U.S. Department of Labor, August 24, 2017.

CHAPTER FIVE

Your Introduction to Investing

I nvesting is a complex activity, but that doesn't mean it requires a complex solution. In fact, the best way to invest is elegantly simple. You don't need to be an investment expert or work harder than everyone else to be a successful investor. To illustrate this point, consider the story of Grace Groner.

Grace was born in 1909 and orphaned at age 12. After graduating from Lake Forest College in 1931, Grace took a job nearby as a secretary at Abbott Laboratories where she would go on to work for her entire 43-year career. In 1935, she invested $180 in Abbott Laboratories stock. Like many people who lived through the Great Depression, Grace was frugal. She bought clothes from rummage sales and she never owned a car. She lived most of her life in a small, sparsely furnished one-bedroom house in a part of town that was reserved for the lowest-class citizens.[1] When she did spend money, she spent it on travel with friends. Those who knew her well said she lived a humble life. When Grace died in 2010, she left an estate worth over $7 million to a foundation benefitting the students of Lake Forest College.[2]

[1] John Keilman, "A Hidden Millionaire's College Gift," *Los Angeles Times,* March 6, 2010.
[2] Aixa Velez, "Secret Millionaire Gives Fortune to Alma Mater," *NBCChicago.com,* March 5, 2010.

Grace didn't apply any advanced investing techniques to amass her considerable wealth. She didn't make frequent changes to her portfolio in hopes of profiting from current market trends. She didn't spend time trying to find the next Apple or Amazon of her day. She didn't move her money back and forth between investment managers in hope of capturing the highest returns. She didn't panic when the stock market was down or try to avoid volatile periods. Grace's success didn't require any of this activity. She simply reinvested the dividends earned from her initial stock purchase and never sold her holdings. These simple actions allowed Grace to avoid the mistakes that plague most investors and fully benefit from 75 years of uninterrupted compound growth on her investments.[3]

Most people think they need to be like Warren Buffett to grow their wealth, but even Buffett credits his financial success to minimizing mistakes and allowing the magic of compounding to work for multiple decades. Need proof? $80.7 billion of Buffett's $81 billion net worth was accumulated after his 50th birthday. $78 billion of the $81 billion came after he qualified for Social Security in his mid-60s. Amidst the thousands of articles and books written about Buffett, it's easy to overlook how powerful the impact of time and compound interest has been on his net worth.

Good investing isn't necessarily about earning the highest returns. It's about doing the same thing for decades on end. The problem for most investors is, unlike Warren Buffett and Grace Groner, they get in their own way. Their own unnecessary meddling in their portfolios robs them of the chance to take advantage of compound growth. The clearest evidence comes from an annual study published by Dalbar that measures how the average investor performs versus the broad market (see Figure 5.1).[4]

Why does the average investor perform so poorly? It boils down to two critical factors: bad behavioral tendencies and investment fees. Once you understand these factors, you can position yourself to invest more effectively.

---

[3] Grace also benefited from a hefty dose of luck. Grace lacked diversification by owning shares of only a single company. Had that company gone bankrupt, she would have been left with nothing.

[4] There are several studies highlighting the investor performance gap. Dalbar's study has my least favorite methodology; however, it is easy for everyone to understand with minimal explanation. If you are interested in learning more about the performance gap, Morningstar's "Mind the Gap 2018" or Ilia D. Dichev's "What Are Stock Investors' Actual Historical Returns? Evidence from Dollar-Weighted Returns" in *The American Economic Review* are excellent resources.

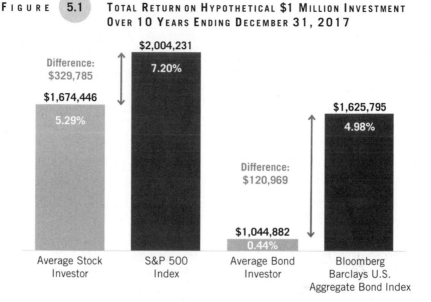

FIGURE 5.1 TOTAL RETURN ON HYPOTHETICAL $1 MILLION INVESTMENT OVER 10 YEARS ENDING DECEMBER 31, 2017

HOW AVERAGE INVESTORS SABOTAGE THEMSELVES

When people follow their natural instincts, they apply faulty reasoning to investment decisions. Throughout our evolution as a species, we've developed cognitive shortcuts to evaluate evidence that requires a great deal of mental energy. Rather than think through a problem, particularly when it's complicated or unclear, our brains prefer to take shortcuts.

These mental shortcuts are deeply ingrained into our DNA, which remains very similar to the genetic building blocks our species developed during the Cognitive Revolution 70,000 years ago. It wasn't until roughly 12,000 years ago that our species began trading in their hunting and gathering ways to live on cultivated land and farms. The Scientific Revolution began just 500 years ago, and that led to an explosion of innovation and advancement.[5] For most of human history, people spent very little of their time analyzing data. Decisions tended to be survival-based, and we carry those tendencies with us today. Unfortunately, survival-based logic usually results in poor investment behavior.

When the market goes down, our human fear instinct kicks in and makes us feel the need to do something. When our ancient ancestors heard

[5] Yuval Noah Harari, *Sapiens: A Brief History of Humankind* (New York: HarperCollins, 2015).

FIGURE   5.2   THE EMOTIONAL INVESTMENT CYCLE

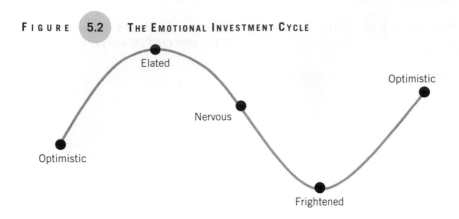

a rustle in the bushes, they ran out of fear. They didn't have time to calculate the probability that the noise in the bushes was a lion. If it was, taking the time to think about it posed too much of a risk of being pounced on. Better to get away first and evaluate later. Thankfully, most of us no longer need to worry about being hunted down by lions, but that instinct to react when we feel threatened remains.

Markets go up and down. Logically, we can know that in advance. But emotionally, we have a hard time staying calm and reasonable when markets behave in a way that makes us concerned about our wealth. On the other hand, we also have a hard time staying calm and reasonable when the market gets us excited about increasing our wealth. Reacting to current market conditions—whether they are good or bad—leads to poor investment decisions.

Most people have heard that investors should want to buy low and sell high. However, investors often do the exact opposite when they get stuck in the emotional investment cycle. Figure 5.2 shows what happens when you invest based on the way you feel instead of systematically investing according to a plan based on evidence.

Daniel Kahneman and Amos Tversky found that we feel the pain of a loss about twice as much as we feel the pleasure of the same sized gain.[6] This behavioral tendency, known as loss aversion, causes us to make poor decisions as a consequence of trying to avoid feeling pain. Falling prices make us nervous and fearful, which results in the desire to get out of investments that are losing money. Similarly, rising assets tend to evoke feelings

[6]Amos Tversky and Daniel Kahneman, "Choices, Values, and Frames," *American Psychologist* 39, no. 4, 341–350, 1984.

FIGURE **5.3**   **MONEY FLOWING IN AND OUT OF U.S. STOCK FUNDS COMPARED TO THE PRIOR 12 MONTHS OF MARKET PERFORMANCE (2000–2017)**

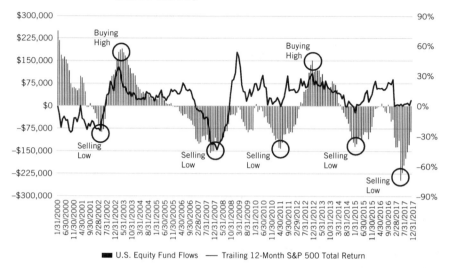

■ U.S. Equity Fund Flows   —— Trailing 12-Month S&P 500 Total Return

of excitement, which makes us want to buy at high prices to avoid the regret of missing out.

Figure 5.3 illustrates this tendency by comparing investor activity to market performance. The black line represents the previous 12 months of market performance (as represented by the S&P 500) and the gray bars represent money flowing into stock mutual funds and exchange-traded funds (ETFs).[7] As you can see, investors consistently add to stock positions when the market is up and sell stock positions when the market is down—this is exactly the opposite of what they should do.

To quote Warren Buffett: "Be fearful when others are greedy and greedy when others are fearful." When markets are falling, we should be excited about paying less for the shares of publicly traded companies in the same way that we are excited to buy clothes, appliances, electronics,

---

[7]The data for mutual fund and exchange-traded funds (ETFs) flows comes from Investment Company Institute. The period from 2000–2009 uses U.S. equity mutual fund data, while the period from 2010 through 2017 uses data from mutual funds and ETFs. This adjustment is necessary because the growing popularity of ETFs in the current decade results in a net outflow in U.S. equity mutual funds for nearly every rolling 12-month period beginning in 2010. However, some of this money flowing out of U.S. equity mutual funds have been flowing into U.S. equity ETFs. The combined mutual fund and equity data from Investment Company Institute begins in January 2010.

or produce that go on sale. But when stock prices go on sale—and that's exactly what's happening when the market goes down because stocks become cheaper—our aversion to losses make it difficult to be a buyer and often results in us being a seller.

Staying disciplined through rising and falling markets is a challenge, but it's crucial for long-term success. Markets provide attractive returns over the long term in exchange for staying invested throughout periods of good and bad performance. Moving in and out of the market results in lower returns and interrupts the power of compounding.

WHY YOU MUST AVOID PERFORMANCE CHASING

Another common error among investors that hurts returns is the tendency to favor investments that have recently performed well. Unfortunately, past performance offers no indication of future results. This universal truth is so important that investment managers and fund companies are required to put that disclosure on any advertisement or educational product that uses past performance. Despite this disclaimer, investors routinely engage in what is referred to as performance chasing.

The performance chasing nature of investors can be explained by several behavioral biases. One of the mental shortcuts we use to evaluate information is recalling the most recent and readily available information stored in our brains, which causes us to place too much emphasis on the recent past. This is our recency bias at work and it's a likely cause of investors' preference for owning investments with the best recent performance.

Overconfidence is another bias that can tempt investors into chasing the hottest-performing investment. Overconfidence has many implications for investors, but the tendency for investors to overestimate their own abilities of understanding the past and predicting the future often leads to performance chasing.

Performance chasing is also the result of our herding bias. Investors find comfort in following their peers, which can lead to investors buying high as they crowd into the most popular areas of the market and selling low as they follow the herd to the exit when prices begin falling.

Figure 5.4 ranks the annual performance of major asset classes in the U.S. and international markets since 2000. As you can see, there is little predictability in asset class performance from one year to the next. Nevertheless, investors routinely make adjustments to their portfolio to seek out the recent winners.

Figure 5.4 Total Returns of Different Asset Classes Since 2000

2000	2001	2002	2003	2004	2005	2006	2007	2008	2009	2010	2011	2012	2013	2014	2015	2016	2017
REITs 31.0%	REITs 12.3%	U.S. Bonds 10.3%	Emerging Markets 55.8%	REITs 33.2%	Emerging Markets 34.0%	REITs 36.0%	Emerging Markets 39.4%	Global Bonds 8.0%	Emerging Markets 78.5%	REITs 28.1%	REITs 9.4%	Emerging Markets 18.2%	U.S. Small Stocks 38.8%	REITs 32.0%	REITs 4.5%	U.S. Small Stocks 21.3%	Emerging Markets 37.3%
U.S. Bonds 11.6%	U.S. Bonds 8.4%	Global Bonds 6.9%	U.S. Small Stocks 47.3%	Emerging Markets 25.6%	REITs 13.8%	Emerging Markets 32.1%	International Stocks 11.2%	U.S. Bonds 5.2%	International Stocks 31.8%	U.S. Small Stocks 26.9%	U.S. Bonds 7.8%	International Stocks 17.3%	U.S. Large Stocks 32.4%	U.S. Large Stocks 13.7%	Global Bonds 1.6%	U.S. Large Stocks 12.0%	International Stocks 25.0%
Global Bonds 9.6%	Global Bonds 6.1%	REITs 3.6%	International Stocks 38.6%	International Stocks 20.2%	International Stocks 13.5%	International Stocks 26.3%	U.S. Bonds 7.0%	Cash 1.6%	REITs 28.5%	Emerging Markets 18.9%	Global Bonds 4.1%	REITs 17.1%	International Stocks 22.8%	Global Bonds 9.8%	U.S. Large Stocks 1.4%	Emerging Markets 11.2%	U.S. Large Stocks 21.8%
Cash 5.9%	Cash 3.8%	Cash 1.6%	REITs 36.2%	U.S. Small Stocks 18.3%	Global Bonds 5.7%	U.S. Small Stocks 18.4%	U.S. Large Stocks 5.5%	U.S. Small Stocks -33.8%	U.S. Small Stocks 27.2%	U.S. Large Stocks 15.1%	U.S. Large Stocks 2.1%	U.S. Small Stocks 16.4%	Global Bonds 1.4%	U.S. Bonds 6.0%	U.S. Bonds 0.6%	REITs 6.7%	U.S. Small Stocks 14.6%
U.S. Small Stocks -3.0%	U.S. Small Stocks 2.6%	Emerging Markets -6.2%	U.S. Large Stocks 28.7%	U.S. Large Stocks 10.9%	U.S. Large Stocks 4.9%	U.S. Large Stocks 15.8%	Global Bonds 4.9%	U.S. Large Stocks -37.0%	U.S. Large Stocks 26.5%	International Stocks 7.8%	Cash 0.0%	U.S. Large Stocks 16.0%	REITs 1.2%	U.S. Small Stocks 4.9%	Cash 0.0%	Global Bonds 5.1%	REITs 3.8%
U.S. Large Stocks -9.1%	Emerging Markets -2.6%	International Stocks -15.9%	U.S. Bonds 4.1%	Global Bonds 5.2%	U.S. Small Stocks 4.6%	Cash 4.8%	Cash 4.7%	REITs -39.2%	U.S. Bonds 5.9%	U.S. Bonds 6.5%	U.S. Small Stocks -4.2%	Global Bonds 5.5%	Cash 0.0%	Cash 0.0%	International Stocks -0.8%	U.S. Bonds 2.6%	U.S. Bonds 3.5%
International Stocks -14.2%	U.S. Large Stocks -11.9%	U.S. Small Stocks -20.5%	Global Bonds 1.9%	U.S. Bonds 4.3%	Cash 3.0%	U.S. Bonds 4.3%	U.S. Small Stocks -1.6%	International Stocks -43.4%	Global Bonds 2.4%	Global Bonds 2.5%	International Stocks -12.1%	U.S. Bonds 4.2%	U.S. Bonds -2.0%	Emerging Markets -2.2%	U.S. Small Stocks -4.4%	International Stocks 1.0%	Global Bonds 2.1%
Emerging Markets -30.8%	International Stocks -21.4%	U.S. Large Stocks -22.1%	Cash 1.0%	Cash 1.2%	U.S. Bonds 2.4%	Global Bonds 3.1%	REITs -17.6%	Emerging Markets -53.3%	Cash 0.1%	Cash 0.1%	Emerging Markets -18.4%	Cash 0.1%	Emerging Markets -2.6%	International Stocks -4.9%	Emerging Markets -14.9%	Cash 0.2%	Cash 0.8%

As we will learn in Chapter 7, the best tools for combating performance chasing are diversification and rebalancing. Having a well-diversified portfolio means creating a predetermined mix of the various asset classes in Figure 5.4 that is based specifically on the goals you are working toward. Rebalancing is the systematic process of maintaining that predetermined mix of stocks and bonds so that you don't fall victim to performance chasing.

THE IMPACT OF INVESTMENT FEES

Even if you exhibit perfect investment behavior throughout your lifetime, investment fees will still constantly work against you by lowering the rate at which your investments compound. To understand how this happens, you must first understand the most common vehicles people use for investing their money: mutual funds and ETFs.

A mutual fund is an investment vehicle that pools money from many investors with the purpose of investing in securities such as stocks or bonds. Mutual funds are operated by professional money managers who invest a fund's assets according to their stated objectives. Each mutual fund shareholder proportionally shares the gains and losses of the fund. The primary benefit of mutual funds is that they provide easy access to a professionally managed set of diversified securities. For example, you can get exposure to the total U.S. stock market purchasing a single mutual fund rather than having to buy over 3,600 individual stocks and make daily transactions to keep their weights in balance.

Without getting into the nitty gritty—because becoming an expert in this space will distract you from what's important to successful investing—an ETF is very similar to a mutual fund in that you get access to a professionally managed portfolio of securities in a single transaction. Unlike mutual funds that trade only once a day at a price equal to your share of the underlying securities, ETFs trade throughout the day and the price can vary from the underlying holdings.

Both mutual funds and ETFs charge fees. The most commonly used gauge of fund expenses is the expense ratio, which measures operating expenses relative to the total value of the fund. Operating expenses consist of the fund manager's fee, marketing costs, custodial services, record keeping, taxes, legal expenses, accounting fees, and more. Shareholders pay these operating expenses on a daily basis through an automatic reduction in the price of the fund. That's right: you're never sent a bill, but you pay fund expenses every day.

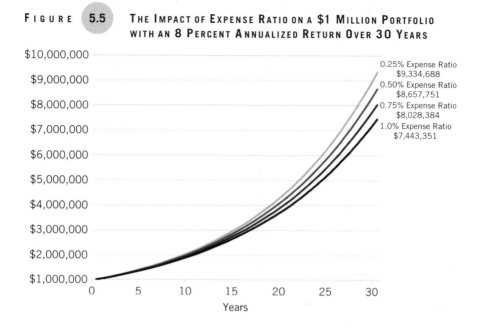

FIGURE **5.5**   THE IMPACT OF EXPENSE RATIO ON A $1 MILLION PORTFOLIO
WITH AN 8 PERCENT ANNUALIZED RETURN OVER 30 YEARS

Automatic reductions in the price of the fund each day is a big reason fund expenses go unnoticed. While compounding works in your favor when it comes to returns, Figure 5.5 shows the same exact compounding effect works against you with fees. To borrow a line from Nobel Laureate William Sharpe: "The smaller a fund's expense ratio, the better the results obtained by its stockholders." That's because the less you pay, the more of a fund's return you keep.

At the end of 2017, the average expense ratio across all mutual funds and exchange-traded products was 0.52 percent.[8] If your portfolio costs more than 0.52 percent, then you can objectively say you are paying above average fees. However, the bar should be set higher (or in the case of costs, lower). In general, you shouldn't pay more than 0.25 percent in fund expenses for a globally diversified portfolio of stocks and bonds. This isn't a scientific number, but rather is based on my professional experience evaluating various types of investments on a daily basis.

Investment fees have been steadily falling for more than a decade, so it is fair to assume my acceptable level of fees will fall over time as well. With regards to most products you consume, people commonly say, "You get what you pay for." With investing, you get what you don't pay for.

[8]Morningstar's Annual U.S. Fund Fee Study (April 26, 2018).

HOW TO CREATE LONG-TERM FINANCIAL SUCCESS WITH YOUR INVESTMENTS

The average investor tends to underperform the market, but you can avoid their fate by keeping costs low and implementing a simple investment process that leverages automation so that you avoid reacting to various market conditions. But even the perfect portfolio and an automated process will feel uncomfortable on a regular basis. It's difficult to remain disciplined through rising and falling markets. I believe it helps to understand the power of markets as well as the relationship between risk and return.

The next few chapters focus just as much on the "why" as the "how" of successful investing. While you may feel ready for the "how" to invest, skipping the theory is like playing a board game without ever learning the rules. There are some important rules of investing, and I want to help make sure you're set up to win. As you learn the rules to the game, you'll be better equipped to deal with the inevitable adversity you face as an investor.

CHAPTER SIX

Harnessing the Power of Markets

My father-in-law, Tom, is the king of buying and selling used cars. Every few years he sells his car and buys another used car. If he doesn't come out ahead every time, he seems to at least break even. It's incredible. Meanwhile, I've only purchased one used car in my life and I felt uncomfortable throughout the entire process. For years, I've been using Tom and his cars as an example of how markets work.

For example, let's say Tom offers to buy my car for $10,000 and then sells it to my neighbor Bill for $20,000. In this scenario, Tom doubles his money overnight. But Tom might not be able to make that kind of profit if Bill and I have access to market data on used car pricing. Thanks to the Internet, I could see that cars like mine sell for $19,000 to $21,000. Maybe I need cash fast, so I agree to sell Tom the car for $19,000. If I had more time to be patient, then I could probably find a buyer willing to pay more.

Tom then goes to Bill, who sees online that the most recent transaction for a car of my make and model was $19,000. Bill isn't in a hurry to buy a car, so he won't buy a car from Tom for $20,000. Instead, Bill chooses to wait until someone sells him one for $19,000 or until Tom drops the price. There are more buyers and sellers in the used car market than just Tom, Bill, and me. If there are lots of sellers and a shortage of buyers, Bill will likely buy the car for a lower price. If Tom holds the only car and there are many buyers, he'll have the leverage to sell at a higher price.

This example demonstrates a market in which participants with different objectives and varying levels of information set prices through the basic forces of supply and demand. The more people participating in a market, the more information that gets incorporated into price. Tom had a better chance of earning a large profit when Bill and I were the only other participants, particularly if we didn't have information from the Internet at our disposal. But if more buyers and sellers of used cars enter the market, Tom will have less of an opportunity to make a big profit.

Financial markets work the same way. The more market participants, the more likely the forces of supply and demand move prices toward a fair value. The chances of profiting from a buy or sell decision are better when there are fewer participants with less information. Another important takeaway as it relates to investing is that every time you buy or sell an investment, you should remember that there is another person or entity on the other side of the trade that may have superior information.

Rather than compete with the market, we can make it work for you. That means understanding supply and demand, the wisdom of the crowds, and the issues with trying to outsmart the market. With this information, you can invest knowing you're building wealth in a smart, strategic way.

BACK TO BASICS: PRICE AND THE INFLUENCE OF SUPPLY AND DEMAND

Markets are at work all around us. If my used car example is too intangible, or too theoretical, then consider something as simple as grocery shopping. When I visit the grocery store, I usually buy some kind of fruit depending on the prices. My favorite is raspberries, which vary in price throughout the year depending on supply. In the winter, raspberry prices often rise to $5 because there is less supply. At that price, I usually opt for another type of fruit, but raspberries are obviously worth $5 to somebody (otherwise the grocery store wouldn't price them that way). If raspberry prices fall to $3 in the winter, then I'm probably going to buy. And during those few magical weeks in the summer when raspberries sell for $1 per pint, I stockpile as many pints that I feel can be eaten before they spoil.

When I make my purchase decision, I never question whether the price is accurate. The price is set according to supply and demand. In the summer months when supply is high, price is low. In the winter months when supply is low, the price tends to be higher. If raspberries aren't selling and the product is nearing the end of its shelf life, the grocery store marks down prices to entice buyers like myself to purchase them. The daily price of raspberries varies based on buyer and seller expectations of market forces.

People tend to respect the power of supply and demand in markets in their everyday life, but that respect seems to break down when it comes to financial markets. At one point or another, nearly every investor makes the mistake of trying to beat the market. Maybe they buy shares of an individual stock, like Amazon or Apple. Maybe they sell a portion of their portfolio in anticipation of a market decline. Maybe they wait to invest cash because they feel the market is overvalued. Maybe they buy an actively managed mutual fund that promises to deliver above-average returns or protect against market declines. These are all examples of competing with the market. Most investors who take this route underestimate the competition within financial markets and overestimate the opportunity for above-average returns.

THE COLLECTIVE KNOWLEDGE OF FINANCIAL MARKETS

Francis Galton, mathematician and cousin of Charles Darwin, first documented the collective knowledge of crowds in an experiment he ran in 1906. Galton ushered a cow around a fair asking butchers to estimate the cow's weight. He found that the average of all the butchers' guesses came very close to the actual weight of the cow. Galton then wondered if the butchers' experience with cattle gave them some kind of advantage in guessing the correct weight, and if the average person's guess would be worse. So he proceeded to ask nonbutchers to guess the weight of the cow. The average guess of the nonbutchers was also remarkably close to the average.

This study was replicated by NPR's Planet Money podcast team. In 2015, they posted a picture of a cow named Penelope and asked people to guess how much she weighed. When they took the average of the 17,205 responses, the average guess was 1,287 pounds. The actual weight was 1,355 pounds, so the crowd's guess was off by only 5 percent.[1]

Famed economist Jack Treynor ran a similar series of experiments with his graduate-level math class.[2] He asked 56 students to guess how many jelly beans were in a jar. The average of everyone's guess was 871 and the actual amount of beans in the jar was 850. The group was only a little

[1] Jacob Goldstein and David Kestenbaum, "How Much Does This Cow Weigh?" *NPR Planet Money,* August 7, 2015.
[2] Jack L. Treynor, "Market Efficiency and the Bean Jar Experiment," *Financial Analysts Journal* 43, no. 3 (May–June 1987): 50–53.

more than 2 percent off the correct value. Treynor repeated this experiment several more times with different-sized containers, but always found that the average guess was remarkably close to the actual number. Additional versions of this experiment conducted by other parties show the same outcome.

How are groups of people able to closely estimate a cow's weight or the number of jelly beans in a jar? Each person's guess has two parts: information and error. In the example of Penelope the cow, maybe people knew the average weight of the cow or based their guess off the cow's relative size to their own weight ("that cow looks about 10 times my size"). With the jelly beans, students might have done complex estimates of the jar's volume by estimating the dimensions of the jar and an individual jelly bean. Lazier students may have guessed based on a gut feeling rather than any calculation.

In each case, everyone's guess was somewhat flawed. But when you get a large enough group of diverse, independent opinions, the errors in those opinions tend to offset each other. That leaves the second part of every person's guess: information. The same thing happens in the global stock market, where prices reflect the buying and selling by millions of market participants incorporating all known information about a company. These market participants are highly educated and highly motivated, so information is quickly incorporated into prices.

In 2017, the global stock market had 76.5 million trades per day worth $441 billion. Investment firms collectively pour billions of dollars into research budgets to improve the information going into investment decisions. Their trading floors are littered with PhDs and CFA Charterholders armed with Bloomberg terminals giving them access to more data than you can imagine. Some well-funded outfits go even further to secure non-traditional data sources such as satellite imagery of farmland, forests, and oil tankers. The most creative approach I've witnessed is a group developing mobile gaming apps exclusively for truck drivers to extract information about shipments and inventory that is otherwise unavailable to the public.

All of this should make the point that the collective knowledge of financial markets incorporates a lot of information into prices. Even more, prices adjust almost instantaneously to new information. By the time you read about a corporate action or economic trend, the market has already incorporated that information into the price of relevant securities. Making an investment decision based on your perception of an investment being overvalued or undervalued means actively competing with the combined knowledge of intelligent, diligent, objective, motivated, and well-financed market participants.

The odds of any investor, novice or professional, consistently out-smarting the market are very slim. That doesn't mean you shouldn't invest, but this information should signal that actively trying to beat the market isn't a smart strategy if you want to focus on building wealth over the long term.

ACTIVE VERSUS PASSIVE INVESTMENT MANAGEMENT: WHICH WINS?

Conventional investing relies on an active investment approach that claims to predict the future and eschews the accuracy of market pricing. For example, a traditional active mutual fund manager buys securities he or she expects to do well in the future and sells securities that aren't expected to perform well. However, the wisdom of crowds tells us that markets are highly efficient and consistently profiting from mispriced securities is unlikely. In a moment, you will see that historical data further supports that active market timing and security selection is a losing approach.

Another approach is commonly referred to as passive investing. Unlike traditional active management, passive investing accepts that market prices are very close to accurate and that you can't systematically profit from potential inaccuracies. Rather than buy and sell stocks to outsmart the market, passive investing uses a rules-based approach that removes the element of human error and emotion that plagues active managers. As an added bonus, funds implementing a rules-based strategy charge lower fees. The most common form of passive investing is using index funds that buy and hold all stocks (or bonds) in a specific part of the global market.

The S&P Indices Versus Active (SPIVA) Scorecard serves as the investment industry's de facto measure of who is winning between traditional active investing and passive index investing. The SPIVA 2017 year-end report showed 84 percent of all U.S. equity funds trailed their respective benchmarks over a 15-year period.[3] Figures 6.1 and 6.2 break down the data by specific categories and show the percentage of active managers failing to beat their respective indices.[4]

The failure of active management demonstrates why it's next to impossible to beat the market. This is a hard concept for many people to accept because professional investment managers are very bright, educated, and

---

[3]I've chosen the 15-year period to capture a full business cycle, but the results are equally dismal over one-year, three-year, five-year, and ten-year periods. Current and past editions of the SPIVA U.S. Scorecard can be found at www.spglobal.com.

[4]Standard & Poor's Indices Versus Active Funds Scorecard, December 2017. Data for the study is from the CRSP Survivor-Bias-Free U.S. Mutual Fund Database.

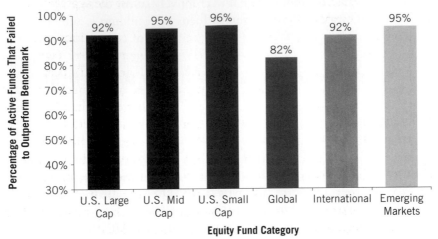

FIGURE 6.1 ACTIVE PUBLIC STOCK FUNDS THAT FAILED TO BEAT THE INDEX (15 YEARS AS OF DECEMBER 31, 2017)

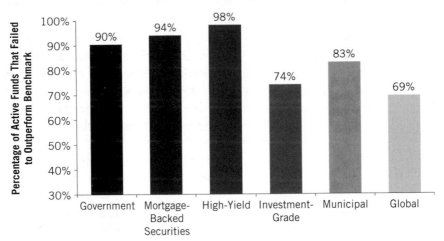

FIGURE 6.2 ACTIVE BOND FUNDS THAT FAILED TO BEAT THE INDEX (15 YEARS AS OF DECEMBER 31, 2017)

hardworking. Throughout our lives, we're taught that better results can be achieved through hard work and superior talent. Go to the gym more often to get in better shape. Study harder to make better grades. Work harder to get a promotion. Train for a race to finish with a better time. All of these statements are generally true. However, investing is one of the rare activities in which greater effort and talent doesn't automatically translate to superior results. That's because you compete against the aggregate effort and talent of everyone in the market.

My favorite analogy for explaining the type of competition you face as an investor comes from Charles Ellis's *Winning the Loser's Game* and involves tennis. Tennis is a head-to-head sport. The world's best tennis player only must beat the player on the other side of the net. Across all professional tennis, there may be a player with a better forehand or backhand. Perhaps there are other players with a better serve or better net game. If the world's best tennis player were to face a Frankenstein-like combination of players with the best forehand, backhand, serve, and net game, he or she wouldn't win a match. When it comes to investing, professional fund managers are competing with a Frankenstein of the highest caliber.

Some investors try to improve their odds by picking managers who have outperformed in the past. Going back to the SPIVA scorecard, we know that some group of managers were winners. Unfortunately, it's not that easy. Research shows that funds outperforming in a given period of time are unlikely to continue outperforming in the future. In fact, the S&P Persistence Scorecard consistently shows that most of the active managers that outperform over a three-year or five-year period perform worse in the following three-year or five-year periods.

Results from the S&P Persistence Scorecard in Figure 6.3 uses a transition matrix to track the performance of top performers over subsequent periods. Among the top-performing quartile of U.S. equity mutual funds over a five-year period ending in 2012, 49 percent of those funds ended up in the bottom half of performers while another 11 percent of funds did not survive. These results are in line with previous years of the Persistence Scorecard.[5]

There will always be active managers who outperform the overall market, but it's extremely unlikely that anyone can identify these managers in advance. Remember the jelly bean experiment? One or two people in the group would have better guesses than others each time, but those people were different each time. The same thing happens with investing, and it's impossible to guess who the next winning active manager will be. Even though Wall Street wants you to think otherwise, research has extensively documented the failure of active management and shown that a passive approach to investing gives you the best opportunity for success.

[5]Current and past editions of the S&P Persistence Scorecard can be found at www .spglobal.com.

FIGURE **6.3** SUBSEQUENT PERFORMANCE OF TOP 25 PERCENT OF U.S. STOCK FUNDS (AS OF MARCH 31, 2017)

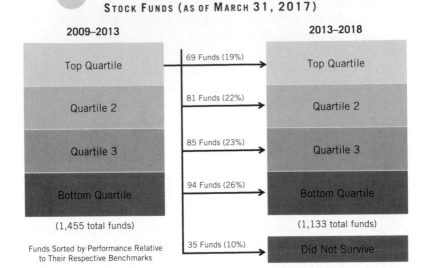

2009–2013

| Top Quartile |
| Quartile 2 |
| Quartile 3 |
| Bottom Quartile |

(1,455 total funds)

Funds Sorted by Performance Relative to Their Respective Benchmarks

69 Funds (19%)
81 Funds (22%)
85 Funds (23%)
94 Funds (26%)
35 Funds (10%)

2013–2018

| Top Quartile |
| Quartile 2 |
| Quartile 3 |
| Bottom Quartile |
| Did Not Survive |

(1,133 total funds)

HARNESS THE POWER OF MARKETS

The highly efficient nature of markets makes trying to beat them a loser's game. Playing it makes achieving your goals more difficult. The good news is you can be a successful investor without playing any games at all by putting the collective knowledge of financial markets to work in your own portfolio.

The first step is to embrace a rules-based approach. A rules-based approach doesn't make predictions about the direction of markets nor does it rely on the ability to pick the best investments. It simply buys and sells assets according to a predetermined set of rules and methodology. Traditional active management takes a forecast-based approach. Not only is forecasting the future impossible and highly susceptible to harmful human biases, but you (or your fund manager) must be smarter than the combined knowledge of financial markets.

The second step is to emphasize a low-cost approach. Costs are one of the few certainties in investing. Traditional active managers have higher fees because they spend more money on staff and research. Fees come directly out of your performance on a daily basis, so the impact is simple: the more you pay, the less return you keep in the end.

Index funds use a low-cost, rules-based approach that eliminates the anxiety and expense of trying to beat the market. Index funds follow a set of predetermined rules for what stocks to buy and how much—specifically, they buy stocks to match the exposure of the index they are tracking. For example, an S&P 500 Index fund buys the companies within the S&P 500 Index so that the fund's gross return is equal to the index return. There's a mountain of evidence showing that indexing is a superior strategy compared to traditional active management.

There are other low-cost, rules-based funds that are often referred to as factor funds. Unlike index funds that give the biggest companies the largest weighting in the fund, factor funds weight holdings according to portfolio characteristics such as valuation, company size, profitability, and price momentum. This allows factor funds to leverage the information the market incorporates into prices and use that information to systematically target areas of the market with higher expected returns.

Successful investing isn't just about the type of funds you buy. It's also about the process for achieving your long-term goals. Even an investor who never makes changes to their portfolio or process still must make a series of decisions at the onset of building a portfolio including asset allocation, investment vehicles, asset location, and rebalancing rules.

So let's turn our attention to these things so that we can design and implement a portfolio that meets your specific goals. We will start that process in the next chapter by explaining the trade-offs between risk and return. As you will see, what looks good on paper isn't always as successful in practice.

CHAPTER SEVEN

Building a Portfolio to Meet Your Goals

You may notice that all my investment examples use an 8 percent return. Admittedly, there's nothing particularly special about earning 8 percent other than it allowed for clean math back when I described The Rule of 72. (In case you forgot, dividing 72 by your rate of return approximates the time it takes to double your money. With an 8 percent return, your money would double roughly every nine years.) But it's worth asking: How do you earn that kind of return in the market?

The primary driver of investment returns is risk. Investing is all about earning a return in exchange for accepting volatility, uncertainty, and the potential for permanent loss. The key is to find the right balance of risk and return by dividing up your investment dollars among stocks, bonds, and cash. This process, known as asset allocation, is the most important decision a long-term investor makes. In fact, the most commonly cited research on the topic determined that asset allocation explains 93.6 percent of variation in portfolio returns.[1] Figure 7.1 demonstrates the impact of asset allocation on returns and variability of returns.

Your portfolio will always rise and fall with the overall market, but the specific mix of stocks and bonds dictates the range of possible outcomes. Portfolios with a greater percentage of assets allocated to stocks

[1] Gary P. Brinson, L. Randolph Hood, and Gilbert L. Beebwoer, "Determinants of Portfolio Performance," *Financial Analyst Journal*, 1986.

FIGURE **7.1**   HISTORICAL PERFORMANCE OF DIFFERENT ASSET ALLOCATIONS OF U.S. STOCKS AND BONDS FROM (1926–2017)

	ASSET ALLOCATION	AVERAGE ANNUAL RETURN	INFLATION-ADJUSTED AVERAGE ANNUAL RETURN	NUMBER OF YEARS WITH A LOSS	BEST YEAR	WORST YEAR
	100% Bonds	5.1%	2.1%	10	29.1%	−5.1%
	10% Stocks and 90% Bonds	5.6%	2.5%	5	28.3%	−6.4%
	20% Stocks and 80% Bonds	6.1%	3.0%	8	27.5%	−10.6%
	30% Stocks and 70% Bonds	6.5%	3.5%	13	26.7%	−14.7%
	40% Stocks and 60% Bonds	7.0%	3.9%	16	25.9%	−18.8%
	50% Stocks and 50% Bonds	7.5%	4.4%	18	29.2%	−22.9%
	60% Stocks and 40% Bonds	7.9%	4.9%	20	34.7%	−27.0%
	70% Stocks and 30% Bonds	8.4%	5.3%	21	40.2%	−31.2%
	80% Stocks and 20% Bonds	8.9%	5.8%	23	45.7%	−35.3%
	90% Stocks and 10% Bonds	9.3%	6.3%	23	51.2%	−39.4%
	100% Stocks	9.8%	6.7%	23	56.7%	−43.5%

have historically earned a higher return. However, those same portfolios with the highest return also experienced the most years with a loss and the widest range of possible outcomes. If Figure 7.1 doesn't resonate with you, Figure 7.2 shows similar information more graphically.

These examples depict the vastly different investment experiences an investor has with various stock allocations. It also serves as a good example that all investing requires accepting short-term losses. For example, both Figures 7.1 and 7.2 show that a conservative portfolio with 50 percent stocks and 50 percent bonds lost more than 20 percent of its value in a single year. That's painful to experience as an investor, but trying to completely avoid losses exposes your portfolio to other risks.

FIGURE 7.2 BEST, WORST, AND AVERAGE TOTAL RETURNS FOR VARIOUS ALLOCATIONS OF STOCKS AND BONDS (1926–2017)

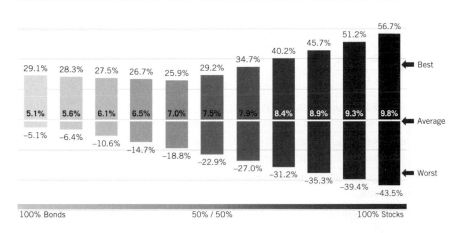

One such risk is not generating high enough returns to meet your goals. Portfolios that don't take enough risk require an unrealistic savings rate relative to your cash flow, and very few people can simply save enough money in cash to meet all their financial goals. A second risk of avoiding riskier assets like stocks is inflation, which may actually outweigh the risk of short-term market losses. A flat rate of 3 percent inflation will reduce a portfolio's purchasing power by nearly 59 percent over a 30-year time horizon.

The goal of investing is to grow your savings faster than inflation without taking undue risks. You can accomplish this through choosing an asset allocation that appropriately blends risk and return. Stocks, bonds, and cash each have distinct characteristics that play an important function in a successful investment plan.

BALANCING THE RISK AND RETURN OF DIFFERENT ASSET CLASSES

By investing in stocks and bonds, you provide financial capital to businesses that use that capital to produce goods or services they can sell for a profit. Stockholders have an ownership stake in a company, which entitles them to the company's future cash flows. Bonds are loans to an entity in exchange for future interest payments and return of principal value. As providers of these two types of financial capital, investors (that's you) expect a return on their money.

Stocks Are Risky, But Essential to Reaching Long-Term Goals

Historically, investors earn a higher return for owning stocks versus bonds. This is commonly referred to as the equity risk premium or the market premium. The higher expected return for stocks is compensation for accepting greater uncertainty and volatility in the price of the investment. Over long periods of time, the equity premium translates into staggering wealth differentials. Figure 7.3 compares these differences in wealth by charting the growth of a dollar invested in stocks, bonds, and cash.

From 1926 to 2017, $1 invested in U.S. stocks expanded to $6,028. During the same period, $1 invested in bonds grew to $97. A dollar in cash increased to $21. In short, historical evidence clearly supports using stocks for long-term investment goals. Unfortunately, it isn't as easy as saying: "I want higher returns, so I'll just own more stocks." Stocks do have higher expected returns, but the day-to-day experience of earning those higher expected returns is far more stressful than it appears on paper. Ignoring risk and focusing only on return increases the chance owning a portfolio that is more painful than you can tolerate.

For example, consider the performance statistics in Figure 7.4 from the same historical period of 1926 through 2017. The 4.8 percentage point difference in returns between stocks and bonds is the compensation you receive for accepting nearly four times greater volatility than bonds and roughly 20 times the volatility of cash. Equally important are the worst one-year and three-year periods. Imagine having all your savings in stocks

FIGURE **7.3** CAPITAL MARKETS HAVE REWARDED LONG-TERM INVESTORS: MONTHLY GROWTH OF $1 (1926–2017)

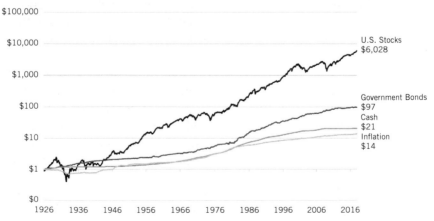

FIGURE **7.4** HISTORICAL PERFORMANCE OF STOCKS, BONDS, CASH, AND INFLATION (1926–2017)

	U.S. STOCKS	U.S. GOVERNMENT BONDS	CASH	INFLATION
Annualized Total Return	9.9%	5.1%	3.4%	2.9%
Annualized Standard Deviation (Volatility)	18.3%	4.3%	0.9%	1.9%
Lowest 1-Year Total Return	−65.4%	−5.6%	0.0%	−10.7%
Lowest 3-Year Annualized Total Return	−42.7%	−0.4%	0.0%	−9.5%

and watching the value of your accounts drop by 65.4 percent in a single year. Even worse, imagine going through a three-year stretch where your accounts lost 42.7 percent each year.

Losses are scary in the moment, and most people can't ride out the emotional roller coaster involved with holding a 100 percent stock portfolio. Stocks are essential to growing your wealth to fund long-term goals like retirement or a child's college tuition, but you need to find a way to balance the risk. That's where bonds come in.

The Role of Bonds

While stocks are the driver of portfolio returns, bonds decrease the volatility your portfolio would otherwise experience. Bonds also experience temporary losses, but the worst bond market losses are not as severe as the worst stock market losses. Figure 7.5 illustrates this point by comparing downturns on the S&P 500 (black line) and the Barclays U.S. Aggregate Bond Index (gray line) since 1990. The shaded areas represent recessions in the U.S. economy.

Taking the data back even further, we can compare returns of the S&P 500 (black bars) and U.S. Five-Year Treasury Notes (gray bars) in Figure 7.6. Since 1926, bonds had a negative return in only 8.7 percent of 12-month periods. Not once did bonds experience a 12-month period with double-digit losses. Compare those numbers to stocks and you can quickly understand the dramatic difference in the volatility between bonds and stocks.

When stock markets experience a sharp fall, bonds act as a diversifier and reduce the overall volatility of the portfolio. The relative lack

FIGURE **7.5**   U.S. STOCK AND BOND DOWNTURNS (1990–2017)

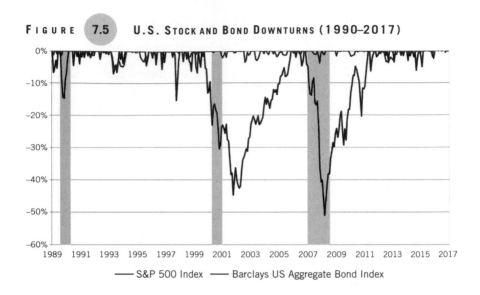

—— S&P 500 Index   —— Barclays US Aggregate Bond Index

FIGURE **7.6**   PERCENTAGE OF 12-MONTH PERIODS WITH NEGATIVE RETURNS
FOR STOCKS AND BONDS (1926–2017)

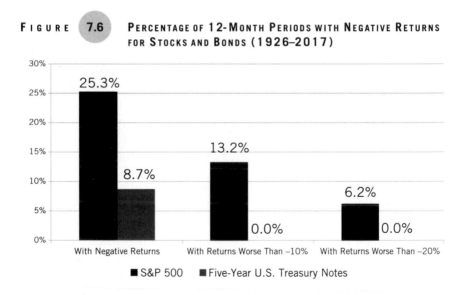

■ S&P 500   ■ Five-Year U.S. Treasury Notes

of volatility is the primary reason to include some percentage of bond
exposure in your portfolio.

What About Cash?

One of the biggest mistakes that investors make is having too much cash
in their portfolio. While maintaining ample cash in an emergency fund or

a strategic cash buffer is important to your financial plan, cash inside your portfolio is problematic for two reasons.

First, cash provides poor long-term returns, which you can see clearly in Figures 7.3 and 7.4. The second problem with holding too much cash is the psychological mind games that come into play. When stocks are going up, investors frequently tell themselves that they will wait for a market decline to use their cash to buy more stocks. But when the prices of stocks do start to fall, investors tend to wait for prices to fall even further before they act. In both cases, you must overcome the desire to invest at just the right time in order to invest your cash.

A nominal amount of cash to cover any investment or trading fees is all your portfolio needs. Your portfolio assets should be dedicated to growth. If you hold more than 5 percent of your portfolio in cash, then establish a plan that minimizes potential market timing mistakes. The best thing is to hold your nose and dive in head first, but you could also plan to regularly invest that cash over a finite period of time.

CHOOSING THE RIGHT ASSET ALLOCATION FOR YOUR GOALS

The way to determine the appropriate mix of stocks, bonds, and cash is to assess your ability and willingness to take risk. It is important to remember that there is no such thing as a perfect portfolio. Assessing your risk tolerance is all about finding the best portfolio for you—the one that you can stick with for decades at a time.

Ability to Tolerate Risk

Measuring your ability to take risk is an objective process. The purpose is to determine how much volatility a portfolio can withstand and still meet your goals. The ability to tolerate risk is driven by your time horizon, liquidity needs, size of human capital, and goal flexibility.

Goals with a short time horizon have less ability to take risk because there is less time to recover from poor short-term performance. Goals with longer time horizons can tolerate bigger portfolio fluctuations because the money is not being withdrawn for many years (if not decades) and has time to recover from temporary losses. All else being equal, as time horizon increases, the ability to take risk increases.

A second consideration for ability to tolerate risk is the liquidity needs relative to the size of the portfolio. For a goal like retirement or financial independence, liquidity needs are the size of withdrawals necessary to meet annual living expenses. Someone with multiple sources of retirement income outside their portfolio can tolerate greater volatility because they are liquidating smaller portions of their portfolios in down markets. Having high liquidity needs relative to the size of the portfolio, however, reduces the amount of loss a portfolio can sustain and continue to fund retirement.

The next factor is human capital, or future earnings potential. The greater an investor's human capital, the greater their ability to take risk, because future earnings can offset potential portfolio losses and volatility. A younger investor with multiple decades of work ahead of them has high human capital. On the other hand, retirees often have zero human capital because they don't generate earnings outside of their portfolio.

Finally, being flexible about the timing or expected cost of goals modestly increases the ability to tolerate risk. An example of high goal flexibility is planning to buy a new car in three years, but being okay with the idea of waiting an extra year or settling for a less expensive model if a bad economic environment reduces your portfolio value at an inopportune time. Another example is with a longer-term goal like retirement. Having higher flexibility with a retirement goal means working longer if the market drops near the planned retirement date.

Willingness to Tolerate Risk

Gauging willingness to take risk is more subjective and difficult to accurately assess on your own. Even the most self-aware individuals could benefit from the expertise of a human or digital advisor (a topic we discuss in more detail throughout Chapter 12). There are few hard and fast rules available, but I can share what I do to understand a client's comfort with risk and how that translates into their asset allocation.

I start by listening to an investor's statements about risk, which means different things to different people. For example, one person might consider the ability to withstand a 5 percent portfolio loss as having a high risk tolerance, whereas another person considers the ability to withstand a 40 percent portfolio loss as high risk tolerance. Other people believe they have a high risk tolerance because they own a small percentage of stocks. In my experience, the more that someone talks about risk or losses, the more risk-averse they tend to be—regardless of their self-assessed risk tolerance.

Reviewing past investment statements can provide clues about an investor's willingness to tolerate risk, too. Was the investor buying or selling in 2008? Does the investor trade heavily in volatile markets? What has the investor's mix of stocks and bonds been over time?

Building the perfect portfolio doesn't matter one bit if it doesn't align with your willingness and ability to take risk. The way you divide up your investments between stocks and bonds will set the tone for the expected range of returns and overall volatility of your portfolio. The more stocks you own, the higher you expect return and volatility to be. Once you've determined the appropriate mix of stocks and bonds, the next step is globally diversifying to enhance your portfolio's compound growth.

LOOKING AT DIVERSIFICATION WITHIN YOUR ASSET ALLOCATION

Nearly everyone has heard the saying, "Don't put all your eggs in one basket." When it comes to investing, you'll want to have several baskets. And you'll want more than just eggs in them. You should have multiple baskets with a variety of fruits, vegetables, dairy products, and meat. In other words, being properly diversified requires investing in a wide variety of assets from across the globe.

While the idea of diversification seems obvious, many investors believe they are well-diversified when they, in fact, are not. The example I typically see is an investor who owns a dozen or so individual companies, but they are highly concentrated in one sector of the market like technology or consumer products. Another common example is an investor who owns a single stock that makes up over 10 percent of their portfolio. Even in a rising market, one company can experience an isolated accident that causes it to file for bankruptcy. Similarly, a natural disaster can strike an industry or region while the rest of the market thrives. While stock investors are compensated with higher returns in exchange for accepting higher risk, it's extremely important to understand that you are not compensated with higher returns for the risk associated with owning a specific company, industry, country, or region.

Other examples of poorly diversified portfolios are harder to spot. For example, I frequently meet investors holding many mutual funds and ETFs across various accounts that feel diversified because they have avoided the trap of owning individual companies. However, a closer analysis often reveals the funds' underlying positions have nearly identical exposures (usually large U.S. companies). To continue our grocery analogy, these investors think their baskets are diversified because they hold cheese, yogurt, and milk. But those are all some sort of dairy product and they lack important nutrients from things like fruits and vegetables. And what about various proteins?

Good diversification is more than having multiple accounts with a variety of holdings. Building a properly diversified portfolio means owning stocks and bonds from all parts of the world, but it also requires diversity in the business types—industrials, health care, technology, financials, consumer staples, energy, and so on. And rather than simply owning the big, well-known companies, we also want to own smaller companies most people haven't heard of before. The reason we want broad exposure to all areas of the market is that their prices are driven by different factors. By combining assets that don't move in tandem, you can further reduce volatility without sacrificing return. To demonstrate how this works, consider the two hypothetical asset classes in Figure 7.7 with very different patterns of return.

Asset Class A (black line) has a return of 20 percent in Year 1, −10 percent in Year 2, 18 percent in Year 3, 25 percent in Year 4, and 5 percent in Year 5. Asset Class B (light gray line) has equally wild returns, but they generally move in the opposite direction of Asset Class A. Combining the two asset classes so that your portfolio holds 50 percent of each generates a dramatically more consistent stream of returns (thick, dark gray line). As a long-term investor, the goal is to combine investments that zig with others that zag to reduce volatility without sacrificing return.

Diversification has obvious appeal from a risk tolerance standpoint, but you're doing more than just managing risk well: you're allowing your portfolio to compound returns more effectively. The math behind this will really blow your mind. Figure 7.8 shows a $100,000 investment in two different portfolios that each have an average return of 10 percent. At the end of Year 3, investors with the High Volatility Portfolio are probably bragging to their friends about earning more than 20 percent returns in each of the past two years. Similar opportunities to brag surfaces with outsized

F I G U R E   7.7   COMBINING INVESTMENTS THAT BEHAVE DIFFERENTLY REDUCES VOLATILITY

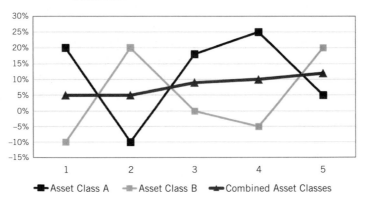

FIGURE **7.8** COMPOUND RETURNS OF LOW VOLATILITY VERSUS HIGH VOLATILITY PORTFOLIOS

	LOW VOLATILITY PORTFOLIO		HIGH VOLATILITY PORTFOLIO	
	GROWTH OF $100,000	ANNUAL RETURN	GROWTH OF $100,000	ANNUAL RETURN
Year 1	$104,000.00	4%	$85,000.00	−15%
Year 2	$113,360.00	9%	$103,700.00	22%
Year 3	$122,428.80	8%	$132,736.00	28%
Year 4	$130,998.82	7%	$118,135.04	−11%
Year 5	$148,028.66	13%	$138,218.00	17%
Year 6	$142,107.52	−4%	$117,485.30	−15%
Year 7	$163,423.64	15%	$150,381.18	28%
Year 8	$178,131.77	9%	$145,869.75	−3%
Year 9	$203,070.22	14%	$176,502.39	21%
Year 10	$253,837.78	25%	$225,923.06	28%
Average Return		10%		10%
Standard Deviation (Volatility)		8%		19%
Compound Return		10%		8%

returns in Year 7, Year 9, and Year 10. But when you look at the end result, the Low Volatility Portfolio ends up with more money.

The High Volatility Portfolio in Figure 7.8 might create more opportunities to brag to your friends over cocktails when it provides outsized returns, but the Low Volatility Portfolio allows you to pick up the check when it's all said and done. The value of diversification is that it smooths the ride, which leads to better compounding of returns.

Remember, time and compound interest are your most powerful tools for success—so let's see how diversification helps you better leverage these tools. Figure 7.9 ranks annual performance of major asset classes and a diversified portfolio by highest to lowest total return. The diversified portfolio uses the same asset classes from the table in the following weights:

- U.S. Large-Cap Stocks 23 percent
- U.S. Small-Cap Stocks 23 percent
- International Stocks 18 percent

Rank	2000	2001	2002	2003	2004	2005	2006	2007	2008	2009	2010	2011	2012	2013	2014	2015	2016	2017	Full Period
1	REITs 31.0%	REITs 12.3%	U.S. Bonds 10.3%	Emerging Markets 55.8%	REITs 33.2%	Emerging Markets 34.0%	REITs 36.0%	Emerging Markets 39.4%	Global Bonds 8.0%	Emerging Markets 78.5%	REITs 28.1%	REITs 9.4%	Emerging Markets 18.2%	U.S. Small Stocks 38.8%	REITs 32.0%	REITs 4.5%	U.S. Small Stocks 21.3%	Emerging Markets 37.3%	REITs 11.4%
2	U.S. Bonds 11.6%	U.S. Bonds 8.4%	Global Bonds 6.9%	U.S. Small Stocks 47.3%	Emerging Markets 25.6%	REITs 13.8%	Emerging Markets 32.1%	International Stocks 11.2%	U.S. Bonds 5.2%	International Stocks 31.8%	U.S. Small Stocks 26.9%	U.S. Bonds 7.8%	International Stocks 17.3%	U.S. Large Stocks 32.4%	U.S. Large Stocks 13.7%	Global Bonds 1.6%	U.S. Large Stocks 12.0%	International Stocks 25.0%	U.S. Small Stocks 7.8%
3	Global Bonds 9.6%	Global Bonds 6.1%	REITs 3.6%	International Stocks 38.6%	International Stocks 20.2%	International Stocks 13.5%	International Stocks 26.3%	U.S. Bonds 7.0%	Cash 1.6%	REITs 28.5%	Emerging Markets 18.9%	Global Bonds 4.1%	REITs 17.1%	International Stocks 22.8%	Global Bonds 9.8%	U.S. Large Stocks 1.1%	Emerging Markets 11.2%	U.S. Large Stocks 21.8%	Emerging Markets 7.4%
4	Cash 5.9%	Cash 3.8%	Cash 1.6%	REITs 36.2%	U.S. Small Stocks 18.3%	Diversified Portfolio 7.1%	U.S. Small Stocks 18.4%	U.S. Large Stocks 5.5%	Diversified Portfolio -25.0%	U.S. Small Stocks 27.2%	U.S. Large Stocks 15.1%	U.S. Large Stocks 2.1%	U.S. Small Stocks 16.4%	Diversified Portfolio 20.1%	Diversified Portfolio 6.4%	Diversified Portfolio 0.6%	Diversified Portfolio 9.4%	Diversified Portfolio 15.1%	Diversified Portfolio 6.4%
5	Diversified Portfolio -2.0%	U.S. Small Stocks 2.5%	Emerging Markets -6.2%	U.S. Large Stocks 28.7%	Diversified Portfolio 13.5%	Global Bonds 5.7%	Diversified Portfolio 15.8%	Diversified Portfolio 5.5%	U.S. Small Stocks -33.8%	U.S. Large Stocks 26.5%	Diversified Portfolio 14.0%	Cash 0.0%	U.S. Large Stocks 16.0%	Global Bonds 1.4%	U.S. Bonds 6.0%	Cash 0.0%	REITs 6.7%	U.S. Small Stocks 14.6%	U.S. Large Stocks 5.5%
6	U.S. Small Stocks -3.0%	Emerging Markets -2.6%	Diversified Portfolio -10.0%	Diversified Portfolio 28.2%	U.S. Large Stocks 10.9%	U.S. Large Stocks 4.9%	U.S. Large Stocks 15.8%	Global Bonds 4.9%	U.S. Large Stocks -37.0%	Diversified Portfolio 22.7%	International Stocks 7.8%	Diversified Portfolio -0.9%	Diversified Portfolio 13.0%	REITs 1.2%	U.S. Small Stocks 4.9%	International Stocks -0.8%	Global Bonds 5.1%	REITs 3.8%	U.S. Bonds 5.1%
7	U.S. Large Stocks -9.1%	Diversified Portfolio -3.4%	International Stocks -15.9%	U.S. Bonds 4.1%	Global Bonds 5.2%	U.S. Small Stocks 4.6%	Cash 4.8%	Cash 4.7%	REITs -39.2%	U.S. Bonds 5.9%	U.S. Bonds 6.5%	U.S. Small Stocks -4.2%	Global Bonds 5.5%	Cash 0.0%	Cash 0.0%	Diversified Portfolio -0.9%	U.S. Bonds 2.6%	Global Bonds 3.5%	Global Bonds 4.7%
8	International Stocks -14.2%	U.S. Large Stocks -11.9%	U.S. Small Stocks -20.5%	Global Bonds 1.9%	U.S. Bonds 4.3%	Cash 3.0%	U.S. Bonds 4.3%	U.S. Small Stocks -1.6%	International Stocks -43.4%	Global Bonds 2.4%	Global Bonds 2.5%	International Stocks -12.1%	U.S. Bonds 4.2%	U.S. Bonds -2.0%	Emerging Markets -2.2%	U.S. Small Stocks -4.4%	International Stocks 1.0%	U.S. Bonds 2.1%	International Stocks 3.4%
9	Emerging Markets -30.8%	International Stocks -21.4%	U.S. Large Stocks -22.1%	Cash 1.0%	Cash 1.2%	U.S. Bonds 2.4%	Global Bonds 3.1%	REITs -17.6%	Emerging Markets -53.3%	Cash 0.1%	Cash 0.1%	Emerging Markets -18.4%	Cash 0.1%	Emerging Markets -2.6%	International Stocks -4.9%	Emerging Markets -14.9%	Cash 0.2%	Cash 0.8%	Cash 1.6%

Diversified Portfolio
Average Compound Return 6.4%
Standard Deviation 12.8%

U.S. Large Stocks
Average Compound Return 5.5%
Standard Deviation 18.0%

U.S. Bonds
Average Compound Return 5.1%
Standard Deviation 3.3%

REITs
Average Compound Return 11.4%
Standard Deviation 19.9%

U.S. Small Stocks
Average Compound Return 7.8%
Standard Deviation 20.0%

Emerging Markets Stocks
Average Compound Return 7.4%
Standard Deviation 32.2%

Global Bonds
Average Compound Return 4.7%
Standard Deviation 2.6%

International Stocks
Average Compound Return 3.4%
Standard Deviation 21.4%

Cash
Average Compound Return 1.6%
Standard Deviation 2.0%

- Emerging Market Stocks 3 percent
- Real Estate Investment Trusts (REITs) 3 percent
- U.S. Bonds 21 percent
- Global Bonds 9 percent

We never know which asset class will outperform from year to year, but the diversified portfolio always falls somewhere in the middle. Over the entire period, the diversified portfolio in Figure 7.9 generates one of the highest returns with just a fraction of the volatility experienced in the other equity asset classes. By owning the winners and losers, the diversified portfolio gives you the best chance of reaching your goals by smoothing out market volatility and improving compound returns.

The behavioral benefits of diversification are as important as the mathematical benefits. You face enormous pressure to change course when an undiversified portfolio does poorly. Of course, diversification doesn't guarantee you will stay the course, but it is easier to ride out a period of poor performance from an isolated part of the market when it doesn't sink your entire portfolio.

INTRODUCE REBALANCING INTO THE MIX

Setting an asset allocation that is aligned with your ability and willingness to take risk is the first step of portfolio construction. Making sure that you are properly diversified within that asset allocation is the next step. Now you need a process to maintain these initial portfolio exposures. That process is called rebalancing.

As we saw for various asset classes in Figure 7.9, periods of higher returns are often followed by periods of lower returns. Rebalancing takes advantage of this trend by selling asset classes that have done well and buying those that have done poorly—in other words, rebalancing ensures you buy low and sell high. To better understand the benefit of rebalancing, consider the diversified portfolio of 70 percent stocks and 30 percent bonds we compared to individual asset classes from 2000 through 2017. Figures 7.10 and 7.11 compare the outcomes of annually rebalancing this diversified portfolio versus never rebalancing.

The annually rebalanced portfolio had a slightly lower return, but it also exhibited slightly less volatility. Most importantly, the annually rebalanced portfolio ended up with more money. As an added emotional bonus, losses during the worst-performing periods for the annually rebalanced portfolio weren't quite as bad as the portfolio that was never rebalanced.

FIGURE **7.10** LONG-TERM PERFORMANCE OF AN ANNUALLY REBALANCED PORTFOLIO VERSUS A NEVER REBALANCED PORTFOLIO (2000–2017)

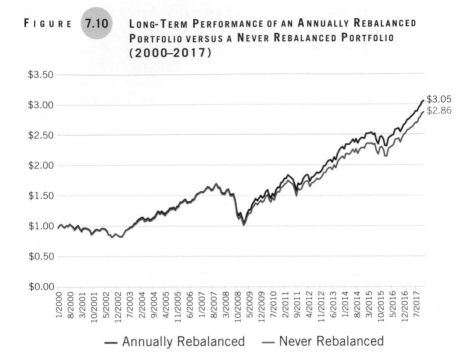

— Annually Rebalanced   — Never Rebalanced

FIGURE **7.11** HISTORICAL PERFORMANCE OF AN ANNUALLY REBALANCED PORTFOLIO VERSUS A NEVER REBALANCED PORTFOLIO (2000–2017)

	Annually Rebalanced	Never Rebalanced
Growth of $1 (2000–2017)	$3.05	$2.86
Annualized Total Return	6.4%	6.6%
Annualized Standard Deviation (Volatility)	10.8%	11.0%
Lowest 1-Year Total Return	−32.0%	−33.3%
Lowest 3-Year Annualized Total Return	−9.2%	−9.8%

There's no guarantee that rebalancing will enhance performance, but the biggest benefit of rebalancing is keeping your risk exposure in line with your risk tolerance. If you set out to invest in a portfolio with 70 percent stocks because it meets your needs, then you don't want to let that portfolio drift to 80 percent stocks as the result of a rising market and become riskier than you are willing or able to tolerate.

Rebalancing on an annual schedule, as was shown in Figures 7.10 and 7.11, is the easiest methodology for investors managing their own money. Another rebalancing option is to evaluate your portfolio on a monthly or quarterly basis, but only rebalance when the holdings deviate from their target weights by a predetermined amount. Financial advisors often implement this slightly more sophisticated approach because they have the benefit of using software to optimize the process. No matter what methodology you employ, it's important to remove personal judgment from the rebalancing process.

We've spent a lot of time focusing on investment theory, including how markets work, the relationship between risk and return, and the importance of asset allocation and diversification when building a portfolio. Now the only thing left to do is setting up automatic contributions to your various investment accounts according to your reverse budget.

CHAPTER EIGHT

How and Where to Invest Your Savings

W ith a good foundation of investment theory in place, you are now ready to implement a systematic approach to investing that will ensure your financial plan fully benefits from the power of compounding. If you built a draft financial plan as you read this book, you should have several things in place by this point.

- You should have goals with an expected value and completion date. These goals should also rank retirement savings and an emergency fund as your top priorities.
- You should have a handle on your current financial situation, including what assets and liabilities you have.
- You should have a good idea of how much cash flow you have available each month to direct toward your goals.
- You should have all savings, bills, and debt payments set up to be made automatically.

Assuming you have done all this work, it's time to begin dollar cost averaging in your investment accounts.

GET STARTED WITH DOLLAR COST AVERAGING

Dollar cost averaging means contributing a set amount to your portfolio on a regular schedule over time. An example of dollar cost averaging is contributing $1,000 to an investment account on the 15th day of the month for a long period of time. This allows you to diversify not just among asset classes, but also across time. When you make equal dollar purchases over time, you buy fewer shares when prices are high and more shares when prices are low.

Figure 8.1 uses a hypothetical individual stock called Lazaroff Lemonade to demonstrate how this works (obviously your portfolio should be diversified beyond holding individual stocks). Say you plan to invest $10,000 a year in shares of Lazaroff Lemonade. In the first year, Lazaroff Lemonade costs $50 per share, so you buy 200 shares. In the second year, the stock price drops to $25 and you buy 400 shares. The shares of Lazaroff Lemonade remain at $25 in the third year, rise to $75 in the fourth year, and return to $50 in the fifth year. In this example, the process of dollar cost averaging lowered the average purchase price of Lazaroff Lemonade. In other words, dollar cost averaging made it cheaper to invest.

While a lower average purchase price isn't always guaranteed, dollar cost averaging is still behaviorally advantageous because investing at regular intervals reduces the risk of buying at the worst possible times and experiencing an immediate loss in value. Investing a large sum of money at a market peak often leaves emotional scars that cause poor investment decisions throughout the rest of your life. Dollar cost averaging doesn't prevent losses—losses are a normal and expected part of investing—but the process allows you to scoop up shares at a discount.

Automating your dollar cost averaging plan removes the need for determining the best time to invest and helps you avoid many of the errors we highlighted in Chapter 5. Dollar cost averaging is also the simplest way to invest paycheck by paycheck with the planned savings from your reverse budget. You don't have to do anything beyond setting up automated monthly contributions to your investment accounts. In fact, you're already dollar cost averaging if you have regularly scheduled automatic investment contributions going to your employer-sponsored retirement plan.

FIGURE **8.1**   HYPOTHETICAL EXAMPLE OF DOLLAR COST AVERAGING

YEAR	AMOUNT INVESTED	PRICE OF LAZAROFF LEMONADE	NUMBER OF SHARES PURCHASED
1	$10,000	$50	200
2	$10,000	$25	400
3	$10,000	$25	400
4	$10,000	$75	133.33
5	$10,000	$50	200
Amount Invested		$50,000	
Total Shares		1,333.33	
Average Cost of Purchased Shares		$37.50	
Ending Value		$66,666.50	

WHAT TO DO WHEN YOU NEED TO INVEST A LUMP SUM OF CASH

While dollar cost averaging is the best way to systematically invest your savings, it doesn't address a common situation of deciding how to invest a large sum of cash. Nobody wants to invest at the wrong time, but you must remember that market timing is a game that nobody can win. So what's the best strategy for investing a large amount of cash? Should you dollar cost average that money over time or invest it all at once?

If we look at historical probabilities, investing a lump sum has a higher expected return than dollar cost averaging because the market is up more often than it's down. In fact, the S&P 500 had positive returns in over 72 percent of 12-month periods from 1926 to 2017. The frequency of positive returns jumps to 88 percent when you look at all rolling five-year periods and 94 percent when you observe rolling ten-year periods.

In 2018, Newfound Research published a more detailed analysis that compared the percentage of periods in which investing a lump sum all at once provided a better return versus using dollar cost averaging to invest cash in your portfolio over time. When comparing the performance of the S&P 500 to bonds and cash over rolling 12-month periods, a lump sum investment beat cash 68 percent of the time and bonds 63 percent of the time.[1] So if you receive a big bonus, inherit money, or slowly build up a large cash position in your portfolio, investing the lump sum gives you the best odds of earning the most return possible. It also lengthens the amount of time you benefit from compounding. After investing the lump sum, you can turn to dollar cost averaging for future contributions to your portfolio.

As we noted in the previous chapter in the context of asset allocation, cash is an extremely inefficient asset for reaching long-term goals. Choosing how to invest a windfall is an important decision, but the fear of making a mistake can make it feel overwhelming. It's tempting to think about the possibility of buying at just the right moment. But here's a dirty little secret that most of the investment industry doesn't want you to know: time is more important than timing.

TIME IS MORE IMPORTANT THAN TIMING

Investment success is more about time in the market than correctly timing market movements. A good example of this comes from an analysis described by the legendary Peter Lynch on the effects of market timing on performance from 1965 to 1995.[2] If you invested $1,000 on the lowest day in the market of each and every year, you would have earned an average annual return of 11.7 percent. On the flip side, if you invested at the market high of each year, your return would have been 10.6 percent. Finally, if you simply invested $1,000 at the start of every year, you would have earned 11.0 percent per year.

Let's recap the findings:

- Perfect market timing return = 11.7 percent
- Worst market timing return = 10.6 percent
- No market timing return = 11.0 percent

There are two takeaways from this simple study on market timing. First, the reward for perfect market timing is very small. It becomes almost meaningless when you consider it's impossible to consistently time market movements over long periods of time. Don't wait to invest if you have a lump sum of money. Simply invest it and keep moving.

Second, investors with both good and bad market timing only achieve these average returns if they never sold in down markets and

[1] Nathan Faber, "Should You Dollar-Cost Average?" *Newfound Research*, February 12, 2018.
[2] *Frontline* interview with Peter Lynch, www.pbs.org/wgbh/pages/frontline/shows/betting/pros/lynch.html.

allowed their returns to compound over time. These returns were not earned by sidestepping the many downturns that occurred along the way. The average includes both the really good times and the really bad times.

One of my favorite investment writers, Ben Carlson, highlights the importance of staying invested through all markets using the fictitious character, Bob: The World's Worst Market Timer.[3] Bob was a good saver, but he only had the courage to invest his savings when the market was doing well. When he was feeling comfortable, he put all his cash into a S&P 500 Index fund that passively tracked the largest companies in the United States. What follows is a summary of Carlson's narrative of every investor's worst nightmare: investing at a market peak.

Bob starts his career in 1970 at age 22 and retires at age 65 in 2013. Bob saves $2,000 a year during the 1970s and increases his annual savings by $2,000 every decade as his salary rises. This means he saves $4,000 per year in the 1980s, $6,000 per year in the 1990s, $8,000 per year in the 2000s, and $10,000 per year in the 2010s until retiring in 2013.

Bob's first investment comes at the end of 1972 after he has accumulated $6,000 in cash at the bank. Unfortunately, the market proceeded to lose half of its value in 1973 and 1974. Bob never sold his investments, but he was too nervous to add additional funds to the market and directed his savings into cash at his bank. It wasn't until August 1987 that Bob felt good about the market again at which point he had $46,000 in savings to put to work. Again, he invested that money into the S&P 500 and, again, watched the market crash in short order. Fortunately, Bob never sold any of his purchased shares, but he reverted back to saving into his cash account at the bank.

The next time Bob felt the future looked bright was December 1999, at which point he had $68,000 of cash savings to invest. His purchase in December 1999 was followed by a 50 percent downturn that lasted until 2002. Again, Bob never sold, but he also made his annual savings to a cash account until his final investment of $64,000 in October 2007. True to form, he invested at the market peak and watched the S&P 500 fall over 50 percent. He was planning to retire in 2013, so he never made another stock market investment and directed his remaining years of savings to his trusty cash account. Figure 8.2 summarizes the purchases Bob made throughout his career.

Although Bob consistently invested at the top of the market, he had two things going for him. First, he never sold his investments despite the

[3] Ben Carlson, *A Wealth of Common Sense: Why Simplicity Trumps Complexity in Any Investment Plan* (Hoboken, NJ: Wiley, 2015), 63–65.

FIGURE **8.2**   INVESTMENTS MADE BY BOB: THE WORLD'S WORST MARKET
TIMER

DATE OF INVESTMENT	SUBSEQUENT CRASH	AMOUNT INVESTED
December 1972	−48%	$6,000
August 1987	−34%	$46,000
December 1999	−49%	$68,000
October 2007	−52%	$64,000
Total Invested		**$184,000**
Ending Balance in 2013		**$1,100,000**

market routinely crashing throughout his career. Even though Wall Street wants you to believe that investment success requires a lot of activity and a complex strategy, it's time and the power of compounding that act as the biggest drivers of building wealth in markets. Like Bob, you are going to experience multiple market crashes throughout your lifetime. Staying invested and making regular investments no matter what is essential to making the power of compounding work for you.

Second, Bob's consistent savings played a huge role in him accumulating $1.1 million by retirement. If Wall Street's biggest secret is that time trumps timing, then the secret that comes in at a close second is your savings rate is more important than your rate of return. The beauty of this secret is that your savings rate is something you control. Much like our lesson about the importance of time, this secret is obvious once you see the math.

FOCUS ON YOUR SAVINGS RATE, NOT YOUR RATE OF RETURN

I recently had the opportunity to meet with a couple in their 30s jointly earning about $350,000. The wife was an attorney and the husband was an engineer. Both had seen substantial growth in their income because of career success, but they hadn't yet taken steps to invest the cash they accumulated. They realized it was time to work with a professional to help develop a plan to more effectively grow their wealth and meet their life goals. This couple, let's call them the Andersons, obsessed over the difference in returns between various asset allocations until I explained that their savings rate was far more important.

For simplicity, let's assume the Andersons are both 35 and want to work until age 65. We will also assume they earn a 3 percent raise each year to keep up with the cost of living, which is a pretty common practice across most professions. Using the long-term historical returns of different asset allocations from Figure 7.1, we can compare the ending balances for the Andersons after 30 years of investing using various asset allocations and savings rates in Figure 8.3.

Your savings rate has an enormous effect on your portfolio. There are a few examples in Figure 8.3 where boosting your savings rate by 5 percentage points is more impactful than seeking higher returns through a more aggressive asset allocation. For example, using a 15 percent savings rate and a conservative mix of 40 percent stocks and 60 percent bonds led to more wealth than a 10 percent savings rate using an aggressive allocation of 90 percent stocks and 10 percent in bonds. Similarly, Figure 8.3 shows a 20 percent savings rate with 60 percent in stocks and 40 percent in bonds finished with a higher ending balance than an allocation of 90 percent in stocks and 10 percent in bonds funded with a 15 percent savings rate.

FIGURE 8.3   HYPOTHETICAL ENDING BALANCES FOR THE ANDERSONS AFTER 30 YEARS OF INVESTING BY ASSET ALLOCATION AND SAVINGS RATES

	ASSET ALLOCATION	AVERAGE ANNUAL RETURN	10% SAVINGS RATE	15% SAVINGS RATE	20% SAVINGS RATE
	90% Stocks and 10% Bonds	9.3%	$6,235,709	$9,353,563	$12,471,417
	80% Stocks and 20% Bonds	8.9%	$5,803,115	$8,704,673	$11,606,230
	70% Stocks and 30% Bonds	8.4%	$5,308,975	$7,963,462	$10,617,949
	60% Stocks and 40% Bonds	7.9%	$4,861,840	$7,292,760	$9,723,679
	50% Stocks and 50% Bonds	7.5%	$4,534,846	$6,802,270	$9,069,693
	40% Stocks and 60% Bonds	7.0%	$4,160,957	$6,241,435	$8,321,913
	30% Stocks and 70% Bonds	6.5%	$3,822,228	$5,733,341	$7,644,455
	20% Stocks and 80% Bonds	6.1%	$3,574,225	$5,361,338	$7,148,450

Savings rate is one of the least-discussed factors in investing, but it's one of the most important topics in investment planning. As a rule of thumb, I believe everyone should seek to save at least 20 percent of their income. It tends to be easiest to save at least 20 percent of your income when you start doing it with your first paycheck out of college, but older savers often need to increase their savings over time.

Sometimes people seek out a higher return portfolio to make up for a low current savings rate, but a better approach is finding a way to gradually increase your savings rate over time. Keeping with our example of the Andersons, let's assume they have been saving only 5 percent of their income, so they create a plan to increase their savings rate by half a percentage point each year. That means the Andersons will have a savings rate of 5.5 percent in Year 1, 6 percent in Year 2, 6.5 in Year 3, and so on. Figure 8.4 summarizes the impact of this savings plan. For the Andersons, increasing their savings rate and using a more conservative asset allocation results in a better outcome than keeping their savings rate at 5 percent and using a more aggressive asset allocation.

FIGURE 8.4 HYPOTHETICAL ENDING BALANCES FOR THE ANDERSONS AFTER 30 YEARS OF INVESTING BY ASSET ALLOCATION AND SAVINGS RATES

ASSET ALLOCATION	AVERAGE ANNUAL RETURN	5% SAVINGS RATE	INCREASING SAVING RATE	ADDITIONAL BALANCE
90% Stocks and 10% Bonds	9.3%	$3,117,854	$6,632,086	$3,514,231
80% Stocks and 20% Bonds	8.9%	$2,901,558	$6,241,076	$3,339,519
70% Stocks and 30% Bonds	8.4%	$2,654,487	$5,790,498	$3,136,010
60% Stocks and 40% Bonds	7.9%	$2,430,920	$5,378,686	$2,947,766
50% Stocks and 50% Bonds	7.5%	$2,267,423	$5,074,738	$2,807,315
40% Stocks and 60% Bonds	7.0%	$2,080,478	$4,723,940	$2,643,462
30% Stocks and 70% Bonds	6.5%	$1,911,114	$4,402,744	$2,491,630
20% Stocks and 80% Bonds	6.1%	$1,787,113	$4,165,274	$2,378,161

The big takeaway here is the more you save, the less risk you need to take to reach your goals. Even without a robust savings rate today, modestly increasing your savings over time makes a big impact. Chances are your earnings will grow over time and you'll pay off debts as you go, too, freeing up more money to be used elsewhere. Figure 8.4 should inspire you to find a way to use that extra cash flow in the future to increase your savings rate.

Much like other areas of your financial plan, automating these increases to your savings rate improves your chance of success. By auto-escalating the amount you regularly contribute to your portfolio, you prevent trying to pick the perfect time to increase your regular investments and ensure you don't let your busy life result in simple forgetfulness.

REDUCING YOUR TAX BILL TO MAXIMIZE YOUR INVESTMENT RETURN

The final step in creating an investment plan is directing investments to specific accounts that minimize taxes and accelerate your progress toward your goals. While most of the investment world has come around to the importance of costs incurred through mutual funds or ETFs, far fewer people consider the taxable implications of their portfolio holdings and trading activity. In Chapter 1, we laid out an example of how taxes slowed the rate of compound growth over the course of a 35-year working career and reduced the ending balance by more than 11 percent. While taxes are an inevitable part of earning money, there are two ways to minimize taxes and supercharge your investment returns: tax-deferred investment accounts and asset location.

Leveraging Tax Advantaged Accounts

Any time you can leverage the power of compounding in your favor, it deserves your full attention. The U.S. government has created a variety of retirement and education savings accounts that allow earnings, income, and capital gains to compound tax-free over time. Lowering or eliminating the drag of taxes means that you can compound your retirement and education savings goals at a higher rate, which in turn makes funding these goals easier to accomplish.

Individual Retirement Accounts (IRAs)

Anyone earning income can open and fund an Individual Retirement Accounts (IRA). As of 2019, you can contribute $6,000 per year, or

$7,000 if you are over 50 years old. Any earnings on your contributions grow tax-free in a Traditional IRA until you withdraw those funds at retirement—at that point, the withdrawals are subject to ordinary income tax.

Some people can also deduct IRA contributions from their taxable income, depending on their tax bracket. Higher income earners won't get a tax deduction, but they still enjoy the tax deferral on investment earnings in their IRA. Unlike a deductible IRA, the original contributions to a nondeductible IRA are not taxed when they are withdrawn—only earnings on withdrawals are taxed as ordinary income.[4]

Roth IRAs

Roth IRAs are a variation on Traditional IRAs (Figure 8.5). The Traditional IRA lets you deduct contributions from taxes today, enjoy tax-free

FIGURE 8.5   ROTH AND TRADITIONAL IRAS: INCOME LIMITS FOR TAX YEAR 2019

ROTH IRA		
Filing Status	Contribution is limited if Modified Adjusted Gross Income is between:	No contribution if Modified Adjusted Gross Income is over:
Single/Head of Household	$122,000 and $136,999	$137,000
Married filing jointly	$193,000 and $202,999	$203,000
Married filing separately	$0 and $9,999	$10,000
DEDUCTIBLE TRADITIONAL IRA FOR INDIVIDUALS COVERED BY AN EMPLOYER PLAN*		
Filing Status	Deduction is limited if MAGI is between:	No deduction if MAGI over:
Single/Head of Household	$63,000 and $73,000	$74,000
Married filing jointly**	$101,000 and $121,000	$123,000
Married filing separately	$0 and $10,000	$10,000

*Individuals or married couples without an employer-sponsored plan such as a 401(k), 403(b), or 457 can make contributions to a deductible Traditional IRA, regardless of income.
**If only one spouse is covered by an employer plan, the deduction is limited if your Modified Adjusted Gross Income is $193,000 to $202,999, and the deduction is eliminated if your Modified Adjusted Gross Income exceeds $203,000.

[4]Income requirements and contribution limitations for IRAs frequently change, but you can visit www.irs.gov/retirement-plans for the most up-to-date information.

FIGURE 8.6 KEY DIFFERENCES OF ROTH AND TRADITIONAL IRAS

FIGURE 8.6 KEY DIFFERENCES OF ROTH AND TRADITIONAL IRAS

	ROTH IRA	TRADITIONAL IRA
Best Suited For	An individual who expects to be in a higher tax bracket when he or she starts taking withdrawals	An individual who expects to be in the same or lower tax bracket when he/she starts taking withdrawals
Maximum Contribution (2019)	$6,000 ($6,500 for age 50 and older)	$6,000 ($7,000 for age 50 and older)
Funded Using	After-tax dollars	Pre- or after-tax dollars
Contributions Grow	Tax-free	Tax-deferred
Withdrawals	Tax-free withdrawals after 5 years and age 59 ½ Tax-free distributions allowed for first-time homebuyer expenses up to $10,000	Penalty-free after age 59 ½ All earnings taxed as ordinary income
Mandatory Distributions	None	After age 70 ½

growth, and then pay taxes on the growth when withdrawals are made in retirement. The Roth IRA is the reverse. You contribute after-tax dollars, meaning that you don't get a deduction on your contributions today, but your money grows tax-free and no taxes are paid on withdrawals in retirement. In other words, a Roth IRA requires you pay taxes today in exchange for not paying taxes in the future.

The best type of IRA for you depends on whether your tax bracket is likely to be higher or lower in retirement than it is today (see Figure 8.6). As a rule of thumb, if you're in a low tax bracket now or retirement is multiple decades away, then you're likely to come out ahead with a Roth.

Employer-Sponsored Retirement Plans

Many corporate employers offer a 401(k) plan to their employees. Meanwhile, educational and nonprofit institutions may offer similar 403(b) plans, and government entities have 457 plans. Much like Traditional IRAs, investors can deduct contributions to these employer-sponsored plans. Unlike IRAs, there are no income limitations on who can take the deduction. Contributions grow tax-free and are taxed as ordinary income when withdrawn at retirement. More employers are beginning to offer Roth versions of these plans, too.

A company-sponsored retirement plan is often the best way to save for retirement for several reasons. First, money comes out of your paycheck before you see it, which removes any temptation to spend it elsewhere. Second, these plans implement a dollar cost averaging strategy that buys more shares when prices are low and fewer shares when prices are high. The automation of the dollar cost averaging within an employer-sponsored retirement plan also prevents you from trying to time the market or deviating from your investment plan when the market environment feels scary.

A third benefit is employers often make matching contributions to these plans. For example, if you earn $100,000 and your employer has a 3 percent match, then you would need to contribute $3,000 to qualify for a $3,000 contribution from your employer. That's a 100 percent return on your money and the only guaranteed way to double your savings immediately.

A final benefit of employer-sponsored retirement plans is they make it easy to create a portfolio with an appropriate asset allocation that is well-diversified and reasonably priced.

Determining the Best Retirement Account to Start Investing

With all these options for tax-deferred or tax-advantaged accounts, where should you start? The following guidelines can help determine the best account for you (see Figure 8.7). The emphasis is on IRAs and 401(k) accounts, but the guidelines also apply to Traditional and Roth versions of 403(b) and 457 plans. Remember, there are income limitations with deductible IRAs and Roth IRAs, but no income limitations for Traditional and Roth versions of employer-sponsored retirement plans.

- Investors who expect to be in a lower tax bracket today than in retirement should save in a Roth IRA and Roth 401(k).
- Investors in their 20s should save in a Roth IRA and Roth 401(k), regardless of current income, because they have enough time for the tax deferral benefit of the Roth to equate to a higher ending balance than deferring taxes with a Traditional IRA or Traditional 401(k).
- Investors in their 30s should consider Roth accounts for the same reasons as investor in their 20s (the long time horizon) unless they're certain their taxable income in retirement will be lower than their current taxable income.
- Investors in their late 30s and early 40s should consider evenly dividing their contributions between Roth and Traditional accounts in a strategy known as tax diversification. Contributing the maximum allowable amount of $19,000 to your 401(k) in this manner would

mean contributing $9,500 to the Roth 401(k) and $9,500 to the Traditional 401(k).

- High-income investors in their late 40s, 50s, and 60s should invest in a Traditional IRA and Traditional 401(k). At this stage in your career, there is less time for the benefits of a Roth to offset the benefits of the upfront tax deduction on contributions to a 401(k) plan. If your marginal tax bracket is below 20 percent at this age, then you should continue using Roth accounts when possible.

Knowing when to stop saving to a Roth account, contributing to a mix of Roth and Traditional, or beginning to contribute to only a Traditional account can be challenging. A good financial advisor can run the math to make the optimal decision. If you prefer to do it yourself, my favorite online calculators for making this decision are www.bankrate.com/calculators and www.360financialliteracy.org/calculators.

A final callout is to people who are self-employed or earning 1099-MISC income. In this case, consider setting up a SEP IRA and contribute the lesser of 25 percent of income (20 percent for self-employed before self-employed tax deduction is included) or $56,000.[5]

FIGURE 8.7   USING TRADITIONAL AND ROTH ACCOUNTS AT DIFFERENT STAGES OF LIFE

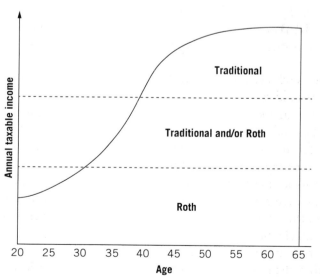

[5] As of 2019. Visit www.irs.gov/retirement-plans for the most current information.

Money paid into this type of plan is tax deductible, and earnings aren't taxed until they are withdrawn. If this formula works against you and you are the sole employee, then an Individual 401(k) is a good option and has the same contribution limits as a typical 401(k) plan. In these cases, I highly recommend working with an independent advisor with experience building and designing corporate retirement plans to select the right option for you.

529 College Savings Plans

Aside from planning for retirement, the most common goal for investors with children is saving for education. There are several vehicles for education savings, but the best is a 529 savings plan. Contributions to a 529 plan grow tax-deferred and withdrawals are tax-free when used for qualified education costs. Many states even offer state income tax deductions on contributions to a state-sponsored plan.

A 529 account can be used to pay for qualified education expenses at eligible U.S. and non-U.S. education institutions including private elementary and high schools, trade and vocational schools, two-year and four-year colleges, and postgraduate programs. Qualified expenses include tuition, room and board, books, supplies, fees, equipment, computers, Internet access, and computer software.

Many of the same benefits that apply to an employer-sponsored retirement plan apply to 529 plans. You can set up automatic deductions from your paycheck or checking account, and those contributions immediately invest in a well-diversified portfolio using an appropriate mix of stocks and bonds. The overall costs of these plans along with the tax benefits make 529 plans far more efficient in saving for education costs than opening up a taxable account on your own or with a financial advisor.

The tax benefits of the accounts described in this section allow your savings to compound faster and ultimately make it easier to fund your retirement and education goals. While the government subsidizes retirement and education savings, it is important to remember that making early withdrawals for nonqualified purposes results in a 10 percent penalty and earnings are taxed as ordinary income in the year you withdraw them. This is to encourage investors to use the money for the purpose it was originally intended.

Asset Location

Different types of investments receive different tax treatment. For example, the interest paid on bonds is taxed as ordinary income whereas qualified dividends and capital gains from stocks are taxed at more favorable rates. Asset location—which is different from asset allocation—seeks to maximize after-tax returns by placing tax-efficient assets into taxable accounts and less tax-efficient assets into tax-deferred accounts. Doing this effectively can provide a significant increase in retirement income.[6]

There is rarely a cookie cutter solution for implementing asset location strategies, but generally, it's best to hold stocks in taxable accounts since the dividends and capital gains realized from these investments are taxed a lower rate than investments generating ordinary income. Bonds and Real Estate Investment Trusts (REITs) make cash distributions to investors that are taxed at the higher ordinary income tax rates and, thus, belong in your tax-deferred accounts such as an IRA or 401(k).

Holding stocks in your taxable accounts also gives investors greater control over the timing of their taxes. Unlike a bond that makes regular interest payments subject to ordinary income tax rates, investors don't pay taxes on capital gains until they sell the security. In other words, you can delay capital gains tax on a stock by choosing not to sell it. From an estate planning perspective, holding a stock in a taxable account can be advantageous because the cost basis of your holdings reset when you die, which eliminates any capital gains you would have realized from selling.

Another advantage of holding stocks in taxable accounts is the ability to harvest losses for tax purposes. Imagine you purchase 1,000 shares of XYZ stock at $100. If the stock price falls to $90 and you sell your shares, then you'll incur a $10,000 loss ($10 loss on each share × 1,000 shares of your stock = $10,000 loss). However, you can use this loss to lower your taxable income in that year and offset future capital gains. The ability to harvest losses for tax purposes is greater when the asset class is more volatile, and stocks are significantly more volatile, and susceptible to losses, than bonds.

If you want to donate some of your wealth to a charity you care about, there's one final advantage to keeping stocks in taxable accounts. Donating appreciated stock, regardless of the size of your donation, is better than writing a check because capital gains on a gifted stock are not taxable to the donor or charity. This strategy tends to be most valuable for stocks in a taxable account since their expected return and potential for capital gain is higher relative to bonds.

The major exception to the rule of holding equities in a taxable account is with Real Estate Investment Trusts (REITs). The majority of return from REITs is in the form of distributions that are taxed as ordinary income rather than dividends, making them less tax efficient than other equity asset classes. As a result, keep REITs in tax-deferred accounts when possible.

In reality, perfect asset location is unrealistic, but you can usually find some opportunities to enhance your after-tax returns. The bigger tax-savvy moves, however, come down to funding the appropriate tax-deferred accounts to help you reach your goals more quickly.

Taxes can take an enormous bite out of your long-term investments and managing that reality introduces a lot of complexity into the task of building your portfolio. The fact that tax laws constantly change makes it even more difficult. Unless you work with the guidance of a financial advisor, I suggest steering clear of asset location techniques because the decisions you make today may not be relevant when tax laws change in the future. The simplest method for reducing the burden of taxes on your investment returns is to leverage tax-deferred accounts whenever possible.

You now have everything you need to build to invest your savings and meet your goals. The investment plan that we've laid out focuses on things within your control: investment costs, asset allocation, savings rates, and your own behavior. Now you simply must have discipline to stay the course no matter what. This is arguably the most challenging part of investing, particularly when markets are falling. In the final investing chapter, we turn our attention to strategies for staying the course when things don't seem to be going according to plan.

CHAPTER NINE

Facing the Realities of Market Downturns

M ike Tyson once said, "Everyone has a plan until they get punched in the mouth." Knowing that you are going to get punched in the face, literally or figuratively, isn't fun. But it does allow us to mentally prepare ourselves to make better decisions after taking a right hook from Mr. Market.

One of the first things to accept as an investor is that you'll occasionally lose money—sometimes a lot of money—on the way to earning a decent return. This is part of the risk you bear in exchange for higher expected returns on your investments. The market will take twists and turns throughout your lifetime. The financial media will dramatize everything along the way making it even harder to stay calm and rational. Meanwhile, the Internet has made access to stock market data and real-time portfolio values increasingly easy, which is problematic because it causes investors to lose sight of the big picture.

LEARN HOW TO HANDLE MARKET VOLATILITY OVER THE LONG TERM

We already know that loss aversion makes losses hurt about twice as much as a similar sized gain makes us feel good—the result is that investors tend to make poor decisions as a consequence of trying to avoid the pain of a relative or absolute loss. Myopic loss aversion is the idea that the more we evaluate our portfolios, the higher our chance of seeing a loss and, thus, the more susceptible we are to loss aversion.[1] Research shows that investors who get the most frequent feedback also take a less than optimal amount of risk and earn less money over time.[2] On the other hand, investors who check their portfolios less frequently are more likely to see gains and, thus, less likely to make bad decisions stemming from loss aversion.

Using historical returns on the S&P 500, there is a 46 percent chance of the market being down on any given day. Looking at your portfolio every day makes the odds of seeing a loss pretty good, which tends to lead to emotions that cause poor decisions. However, if you wait longer and look at returns every month, there is only a 38 percent chance of seeing the market is down. Looking at your portfolio only once a year drops the chances of seeing a loss down to 21 percent. Figure 9.1 shows different rolling periods of time and the historical frequency of a positive or negative return.

The takeaway? Don't look at your portfolio daily. There's no need to do so, and it often leads to harmful behaviors rather than helpful ones. The goals you are investing for are likely several years to several decades away, so it's virtually pointless to review stock market performance more than once a year.

F I G U R E   9.1   ROLLING PERFORMANCE OF THE S&P 500 (1926–2017)

	POSITIVE	NEGATIVE
Daily	54%	46%
Monthly	62%	38%
Quarterly	68%	32%
6 Months	74%	26%
1 Year	79%	21%
5 Years	88%	12%
10 Years	94%	6%
20 Years	100%	0%

[1] Shlomo Benartzi and Richard Thaler, "Myopic Loss Aversion and the Equity Risk Premium Puzzle," *The Quarterly Journal of Economics* 110, no. 1 (February 1, 1995): 73–92.
[2] Richard Thaler, Amos Tversky, Daniel Kahneman, and Alan Schwartz, "The Effect of Myopia and Loss Aversion on Risk Taking: An Experimental Test," *The Quarterly Journal of Economics* 112, no. 2 (May 1, 1997): 647–666.

Think about it this way. Most people would probably agree that look-ing up the value of your home on an hourly, daily, or even quarterly basis would be a silly idea—particularly if you had no plans to move out in the near future. So why check market performance that frequently? It becomes even less sensible when you have a thoughtfully crafted, automated plan for money you won't need for multiple decades. I'm not suggesting looking at your portfolio only once every ten years—although I wouldn't discourage it if you are automatically making contributions and rebalancing—but the worst-behaved investors are those who frequently check the stock market and their portfolios.

The key to maintaining discipline when you invest is ignoring the short-term market movements and related market commentary as much as possible. When things seem unsettling, think into the future and visu-alize yourself living a life in which you've reached all your goals. As you visualize the future, remember that the stock market always goes up and down. While things can seem very frightening in the moment, all crises eventually end.

We never know when or why the next market downturn will happen. What we do know is that market downturns happen on a regular basis. Figure 9.2 details the worst losses for the S&P 500 every year dating back to 1926. Double-digit losses occur in 65 percent of calendar years and nearly a quarter of the time losses are greater than 20 percent. Despite the frequent losses, the S&P 500 earned an average annual return of 10.16 per-cent over this period.

FIGURE 9.2 WORST INTRA-YEAR LOSSES FOR THE S&P 500 (1926–2017)

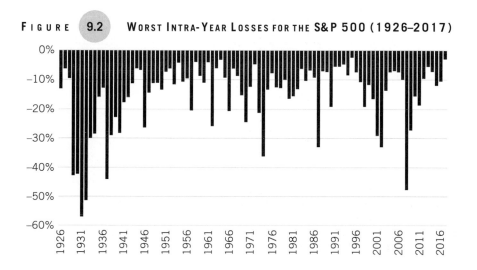

Remember, risk and return are closely related. Losses are the price you pay in exchange for higher expected returns. There is no such thing as a riskless, high return investment (you should run away as fast as possible from anyone suggesting otherwise). The good news is that you can reduce the chance of permanent loss by staying invested over a long period of time. In fact, overall market losses can present a huge advantage to investors who dollar cost average because market downturns allow them to buy stocks at lower prices.

Markets are highly uncertain in the short term. In the long term, however, the range of outcomes narrow. You can see this in Figure 9.3, which compares one-year, three-year, and ten-year real returns (gray lines) to the long-term average real return (black line) on the S&P 500. Stock returns greatly deviate from the average return over one-year periods, but returns tend to smooth out over time. This means long-term investors are better positioned to ride out the stock market's inevitable ups and downs.

Volatility is not the enemy. It's the cost of higher returns. When you accept that the market is very good at incorporating information into prices, you'll see there's no way for people to reasonably predict when and why downturns occur. But we can reasonably expect downturns to continue occurring with a similar degree of frequency in the future. That means we can plan for them—and you're better off planning on downturns occurring regularly than trying to predict when stocks will take a tumble.

Whenever you are feeling uneasy about the market falling, consider how short bear markets are compared to bull markets. Figure 9.4 shows that the length and gains of a typical bull market (black) are disproportionately greater than the length and severity of bear markets (gray). Trying to dodge bear markets means sitting in cash and missing out on the disproportionately greater gains that are essential to meeting your financial goals. Rather than worry about avoiding the relatively short-lived downturns, as difficult as they feel in the moment, you must focus on the things within your control to capture all the returns the market offers in the good times.

Investing is not easy, but good investment behavior is crucial to capturing the market's long-term returns. The key is to put systems in place that deter you from making changes in response to market movements. Automating your investment plan helps by reducing the number of ongoing decisions you make—the fewer ongoing decisions you must make, the less opportunity there is for mistakes.

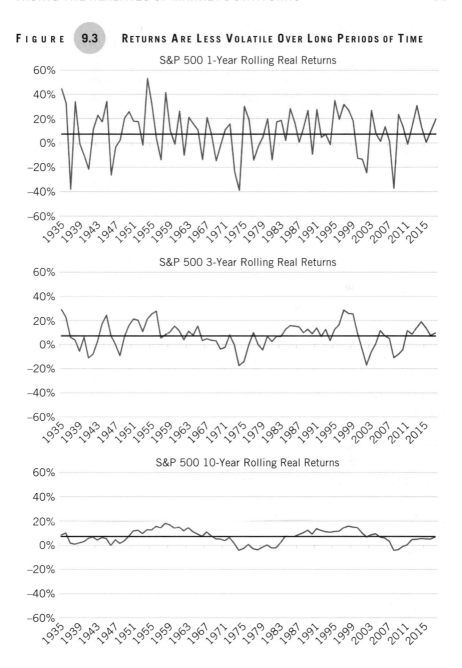

F I G U R E   9.3   RETURNS ARE LESS VOLATILE OVER LONG PERIODS OF TIME

S&P 500 1-Year Rolling Real Returns

S&P 500 3-Year Rolling Real Returns

S&P 500 10-Year Rolling Real Returns

FIGURE **9.4**   U.S. BULL AND BEAR MARKETS (1903–2017)

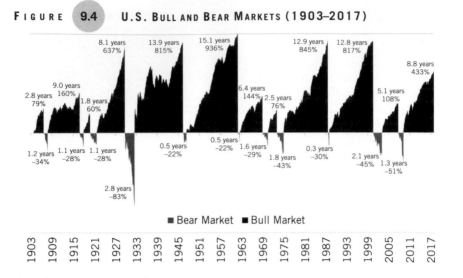

■ Bear Market   ■ Bull Market

FIGHT BAD INVESTOR BEHAVIOR WITH GOALS-BASED INVESTING

Let's not forget the reason for investing in the first place: to compound money at a rate that allows you to reach your biggest financial goals. Breaking down your goals into separate portfolios with unique asset allocations makes staying the course easier. This process, known as goals-based investing, is quite simple.

The **Goal Planning Worksheet** groups goals into the three basic investment time horizons: short-term (less than five years), intermediate-term (five to 15 years) and long-term (15 or more years). Goals-based investing makes it easier to overlook the short-term market movements because they're not relevant to long-term goals. Meanwhile, short-term goals are invested in more conservative allocations for protection against large drops in the stock market.

To illustrate how this might work, Figure 9.5 provides four sample portfolios with low-cost mutual funds that align with the investment philosophy described in this book. Remember, a larger allocation to stocks increases the return you expect to earn over time. In exchange for that higher potential return, you accept greater uncertainty in the short term in the form of price volatility and losses. Goals with a longer time horizon can tolerate the risk of a higher stock allocation because they have more time to recover from temporary losses.

FIGURE **9.5** SAMPLE PORTFOLIOS FOR GOALS-BASED INVESTING

	SAMPLE FUNDS	DEFENSIVE	CONSERVATIVE	MODERATE	AGGRESSIVE
Stocks		20%	40%	60%	80%
U.S. Stocks	DFA U.S. Core Equity 2 Portfolio Vanguard Total Stock Market Index	14%	28%	42%	56%
Non-U.S. Stocks	DFA World ex-U.S. Core Equity Portfolio Vanguard Total International Stock Market Index	6%	12%	18%	24%
Bonds		80%	60%	40%	20%
U.S. Bonds	DFA Investment Grade Portfolio Vanguard Total Bond Market Index	56%	42%	28%	14%
Non-U.S. Bonds	DFA Five-Year Global Fixed Income Portfolio Vanguard Total International Bond Market Index	24%	18%	12%	6%

Whenever the stock market is down, you can rest assured that your short-term goals are invested in a less volatile allocation, while your intermediate- and long-term goals have plenty of time to recover from larger temporary losses that come with the Moderate or Aggressive allocation. When you put it all together, it means less day-to-day worry.

TESTING YOUR PROBABILITY OF SUCCESS

Anytime you feel nervous about the market, you're better off reviewing the underlying assumptions in your financial plan than making changes to your portfolio. It's much easier to tolerate market volatility when you know your financial plan is still on track. One way to do this is through a Monte Carlo analysis.

A Monte Carlo analysis uses information like your current savings rate, monthly contributions, asset allocation, and liquidity needs. These are all things within your control. Using historical data and information about your goals, a Monte Carlo analysis runs thousands of scenarios to generate a probability that your plan will be successful. This can help you thoughtfully craft a financial plan that takes periods of bad performance into account and does so without the emotion you might feel when dealing with volatility in real time. You can spend less time making predictions about the market and more time planning around things you can control.

Remember, financial success isn't magic. It's engineering. Up until this point, I've provided straightforward and actionable steps to build a system engineered for financial success, but running a Monte Carlo analysis probably requires enlisting outside help. There are free options online, but they are flawed and lack robust insight. My advice is to utilize a financial advisor who meets the guidelines outlined in Chapter 12.

CHAPTER TEN

Family Finances

When you are single, you manage finances in a way that is comfortable and that you understand—no one must approve or disapprove of your financial decisions. Married couples, however, must agree on a system for budgeting, paying bills, and saving for the future. It starts with discussing your respective financial situations and expectations, taking stock of what you own and owe, and agreeing upon common financial goals.

Even if you don't have a family, this chapter still has something for you. There's valuable information on buying a home, which certainly applies to a variety of people in different stages of life. The decision to rent or buy a home is one of the most important financial decisions you will make and it's important to get it right.

But first, I will address common questions people face when they get married and have children. Should you and your spouse combine finances or keep them separate? How much money do you need before thinking about children? How much should you save for your child's education? Planning ahead rather than making these decisions on the fly dramatically increases your chances of financial success in the long run.

GETTING MARRIED AND COMBINING FINANCES

Planning for marriage encompasses more than deciding whether to serve chicken at the reception or choosing a honeymoon destination. You'll face the enormous responsibility of combining your personal finances (or not) and reassessing the way you both handle money. The key is learning to proactively communicate about finances and make decisions as a team.

Everyone feels differently about their finances. Different money personalities and levels of income require unique strategies. The three strategies that follow serve as a starting point for combining your finances and can be customized to better fit your situation. (Note that these different money models are intended for couples who are married or have committed to a life partnership. For couples living together who have yet to lock it down, it makes more sense to keep finances separate and divvy up joint expenses as you see fit.)

The most important thing in deciding how to combine finances is to be honest about your feelings from the start and always keep an open line of communication. Money is frequently considered to be one of the biggest strains on marital relationships, but working together to find solutions that work for everyone can reduce some of the stress.

Keep It Simple: Joint Accounts for Everything

Using joint accounts is the easiest way to combine finances. Good communication is essential, so it's important to maintain an ongoing dialogue about money. One way to accomplish this is setting a spending threshold that requires spousal notification. For example, some couples agree to tell each other about purchases greater than $250. It isn't intended to be an approval process whereby the other spouse signs off on the purchase before it's made. Rather it is a way to ensure the lines of communication remain open.

Another way to facilitate meaningful money conversations is reviewing your goals worksheets and financial statements together at least once a year. This will raise important discussions and create opportunities to express money concerns before something becomes a problem. You could also consider quarterly "money dates" to stay on the same page about smaller financial matters.

What's Mine Is Mine: Separate Accounts for Income and Spending

The opposite of merging finances is maintaining separate accounts, which allows couples to divvy up joint expenses and enjoy total freedom over their own finances. Although having similar incomes makes this much simpler, couples with different levels of income can separate finances by assigning more expensive items like a mortgage to the higher earner and utilities to the lower earner. Where things get trickier is saving for retirement or paying down debt.

This is not a set-it-and-forget-it solution because life (and your finances) get more complicated over time. This system requires regular assessments of different assigned expenses, particularly as children enter the equation or career growth creates greater income disparity between spouses. If you prefer making financial decisions that require less ongoing maintenance, then this system might not be ideal for you.

The Hybrid Model: Allocate Income to Both Joint and Individual Finances

Hybrid models allow each spouse to have some money of their own while most everyday expenses are paid out of a joint account. There are two methods for employing a hybrid model. The first is the Percentage Model. Here's how it works: both spouses put 80 percent of their income into a joint account and 20 percent into personal spending accounts they hold separately. The joint account covers everyday expenses like mortgage, groceries, meals together, vacations, medical bills, and long-term savings. Personal spending accounts might cover items such as clothing, personal electronics, accessories, gifts, or trips without the other spouse.

When using a Percentage Model, the 80/20 split is a starting point that can be tailored your personal circumstances. For example, large income disparities may result in one spouse having much more personal spending money. In this case, consider changing up the income split—one spouse might put in 80 percent of income while the other puts in 40 percent.

The second hybrid model is the Fixed Dollar Model, which allocates a specific dollar amount of each paycheck to personal spending accounts and the rest toward a joint account. Say one person earns a monthly after-tax paycheck of $10,000 and the other brings in a monthly after-tax paycheck of $5,000. In this case, both spouses might put $1,000 a month into their personal spending accounts and then pool the remaining $13,000 into a joint account.

The Fixed Dollar Model gives everyone an equal amount of personal spending money. For some couples, this works better than the Percentage Model and reduces the sense of inequality. I've also seen clients choose a variation of the Fixed Dollar Model in which the higher earner from the preceding example puts an extra $500 a month into his or her personal spending account.

The worksheets on **peterlazaroff.com/worksheets** are perfect for exploring ways to combine finances and discuss other family money decisions, including the unique expenses associated with having children. Combining finances with your spouse is a walk in the park compared to planning for children. While the finances of raising a child may seem daunting, incorporating them in your worksheets can make things far less stressful. As you prepare for life with your new child, update those worksheets and make any necessary changes to your existing plan.

WHAT TO EXPECT (WITH YOUR FINANCES) WHEN YOU'RE EXPECTING

Many people believe they need a certain amount of money before having a family, but that isn't necessarily true. Yes, there are upfront costs, but the real expense of children comes from ongoing expenditures such as food, toys, child care, and education. Fortunately, your budget naturally adapts to accommodate new needs because staying at home taking care of a baby means less time to spend money on restaurants, bars, entertainment, and travel.

The best way to prepare for increased expenses is to start making monthly contributions to a savings account dedicated to baby-related costs. Putting aside a few hundred dollars each month gives you a chance to get used to the bigger cash outflows from your checking account. It also provides you with a nice cash cushion for baby-related expenses you might overlook. Whether you are single, engaged, or married, making automated savings towards a designated "Kids" account early is the best way to financially prepare for children.

Similarly, nothing combats the cost of raising children better than a high savings rate. Prior to having children, my wife and I saved over 30 percent of our income. In the years since we had children, our savings rate declined as we redirected savings on our **Cash Flow Worksheet** toward child-related costs. While having children expanded our monthly expenses, the disciplined savings habits we established early in our careers kept our standard of living intact and long-term goals on track.

SAVING FOR YOUR CHILD'S COLLEGE EDUCATION

With children usually comes the desire to fund their college education. There's no denying the benefits of a college education. There's also no hiding from the cost. According to the College Board, the average annual cost of a four-year public college for in-state students is $21,370, while the average annual cost of a four-year private college is $48,510.[1] Those costs have historically gone up by 5 percent a year, so putting a savings plan in place is important. As with all savings goals, the earlier you start saving, the better you can leverage the power of compounding.

Before discussing the best vehicles and strategies for college savings, there are two things to keep in mind. The first and most important thing to remember is that your child can always receive financial aid or take out loans to pay for college, but there's no such option for your retirement. Postponing retirement savings means missing out on decades of tax-deferred compound growth and it may be hard to catch up later. As the father of two children, I completely understand the desire to give your kids everything they need to get the best education possible. My plan is to pay for my children's college expenses, but I will always prioritize my retirement savings. I'm pretty sure that if my children had the choice of taking out student loans or having me live in their basement during my retirement, they would choose to fund their own education.

The second thing to keep in mind is that you don't need to save 100 percent of your children's college expenses by the time they graduate from high school. A good target college savings amount is 70 percent and plan to pay the rest from your cash flow at that time. There are a few reasons why:

- **You can't know that your child will even go to college.** The ideal vehicles for education savings have penalties if you withdraw money for purposes other than education.
- **It's difficult to predict the type of college your child might attend.** Until your child is in high school, it's impossible to know whether their tuition will resemble an in-state school, an Ivy League school, or something in between.
- **Your child may receive a scholarship.** Even though you can withdraw money from a 529 up to the amount of a tax-free scholarship without paying the 10 percent penalty, the earnings portion of your withdrawal is still subject to income taxes.

Now that you know to prioritize your retirement savings and only target to save 70 percent of the projected cost of college, let's talk about the best place to stick this cash for your kids' educations: a 529 savings plan.

---

[1] The College Board: Trends in College Pricing, 2018 (trends.collegeboard.org/college-pricing).

HOW TO MAKE GOOD USE OF A 529 PLAN

529 savings plans offer a unique combination of tax-advantaged features that no other education savings vehicle can match. Anyone can make contributions up to the federal annual exclusion amount, which is currently $15,000 per year for an individual and $30,000 for a married couple filing joint tax returns.[2] Contributions grow tax-free and withdrawals for qualified education expenses are tax-free at the federal level. Qualified education expenses include tuition, room and board, fees, books, and supplies at any college or graduate school that is accredited by the Department of Education. Funds can also be used to pay up to $10,000 of Kindergarten through Grade 12 tuition expenses a year.

If withdrawals are not used for qualified education expenses, the earnings portion is subject to the account owner's income tax rate plus a 10 percent federal penalty.[3] However, money in a 529 plan can be transferred to a different 529 plan once per year without income tax or penalty, which is particularly useful for people with multiple children. If any of your children get full scholarships or have funds left over in the account after graduation, you can also change the account beneficiary to a different family member.[4] Funds in a 529 account can also be transferred to an ABLE account without federal tax consequences. An ABLE account is a tax-advantaged savings account for disability-related expenses for individuals who become disabled before age 26.

Every state administers its own 529 plan, but there is no requirement to use your state's plan.[5] All states allow for automatic contributions into diversified portfolios, but the investment options and costs vary. If you aren't required to use your state's plan to receive a tax deduction or you live somewhere with no state income tax, you can use Morningstar's 529 plan ranks to help select the plan best for you.

[2]Under special rules unique to 529 plans, a lump-sum gift of up to five times the annual gift exclusion amount is allowed in a single year, which means that individuals can make a lump-sum gift of up to $75,000 and married couples can gift up to $150,000 (as of 2019). No gift tax will be owed, provided the gift is treated as having been made in equal installments over a five-year period and no other gifts are made to that beneficiary during the five years.
[3]Visit www.irs.gov for up-to-date rules and requirements for 529 plans.
[4]According to Section 529 of the Internal Revenue Code, "family members" include children and their descendants, stepchildren, siblings, parents, stepparents, nieces, nephews, aunts, uncles, in-laws, and first cousins. States are free to impose additional restrictions, such as age and residency requirements.
[5]The exception here is states that require you use their plan to realize a state tax deduction in the amount of your contribution. Even if you live in one of these states, you don't have to use their plan, but you probably should in order to capture the tax deduction.

Finally, it is important to note that there are two types of 529 plans: savings plans and prepaid tuition plans. A 529 savings plan is the individual account that we've been discussing. The less common 529 prepaid tuition plan is typically something to avoid because of its lack of flexibility. With a 529 prepaid tuition plan, you purchase college tuition credits at today's prices for future use at a limited group of in-state public colleges from your state of residence. That means you may not realize the full value of these credits if you attend a private or out-of-state public school, receive a scholarship, attend a lower-cost community college, or do not attend college at all. The credits also come with age limitations and restrictions on changing beneficiaries. Even worse, prepaid plans cannot be used to pay for room and board, computers, or books.

BUYING A HOME

Owning a first home is an exciting prospect. It has long been part of the quintessential American Dream. While owning your own house comes with many intangible benefits that are difficult to quantify, there are financial aspects you must consider. A house and its mortgage will likely be among the biggest items on your **Net Worth Worksheet**, so the math needs to be taken seriously.

When Does Buying a Home Make Sense?

Whether a home purchase makes sense depends on several financial and emotional factors. The following is a series of questions and exercises that, when answered truthfully and realistically, will help you make an informed decision.

1. **Do you plan to live in the same place for at least five years?**
    If the answer is no, then you should definitely rent. It takes at least five years for a house to appreciate enough to offset the broker fees and closing costs, which can add up to 10 percent of the home's purchase price. The longer you live in your home, the more likely you'll benefit financially from owning it. The following are common life events that can turn an ideal home purchase into a bad financial decision by simply shortening the time horizon in the property:
    *   Getting married
    *   Having children
    *   Going back to school
    *   Moving to a new city
    *   Changing careers

Honestly reflecting on how long you can reasonably expect to live in the same home is an important exercise. Envision where you want to be in five years with your career, family, and financial goals. How does a home fit into these dreams? How would buying a house impact you financially if life turns out differently than you expected? Will the cost or the responsibilities associated with owning a house prevent you from living the life you truly want?

2. **Is owning less expensive than renting?**

This seems obvious, but most people don't evaluate the true cost of ownership versus renting. Comparing monthly rent to a potential mortgage payment misses a huge amount of costs associated with buying a home. Figure 10.1 outlines some of the major monthly and one-time expenses that must be considered to make a fair comparison.

The **Rent or Buy Worksheet** on **peterlazaroff.com/worksheets** estimates the cost of owning versus renting. If you are confident about living in the same home for at least five years, then it's fine to buy a

FIGURE **10.1** ESTIMATED COSTS OF BUYING A HOME

	ESTIMATED MONTHLY EXPENSE
Mortgage Payment	
Property Taxes	
Insurance	
Private Mortgage Insurance (PMI)	
Maintenance (Home Price × 1.0%) ÷ 12 Months	
Home Services (Landscaping, Pest Control, etc)	
Improvements	
Other (Utilities, Dues, Assessments)	
Tax Savings	
Estimated Monthly Expenses	
	Estimated One-Time Expenses
Closing Costs (2% to 5% of Amount Borrowed)	
Broker's Fees (4% to 7% of Home Price)	
Moving Costs, Initial Repairs, and Furnishing Expenses	
Estimated One-Time Expenses	

house even when ownership is more expensive than renting. The key is to make sure the higher cost of ownership is included in your **Cash Flow Worksheet** and doesn't interfere with your ability to meet other life priorities listed in your **Goals Planning Worksheet.**

3. **What are your current and future career prospects?**

Your future earnings are relevant to how a mortgage will impact your life. A general rule of thumb is you should not spend more than 25 percent of your gross monthly income on your monthly housing payment. This will greatly inform the house you can afford, but it also might restrict the career choices you make upon purchasing a home.

Owning a home makes it more financially restrictive to relocate for a job opportunity, go back to school, change career paths, or start a business. If you have a high degree of career uncertainty, renting is a safer choice because it provides greater financial flexibility.

4. **Can you afford the down payment and upfront costs associated with buying a home?**

Whether you are buying a first home or preparing to move into a bigger second home, the down payment and closing costs will take a big bite out of your savings. Review your **Net Worth Worksheet** to identify the assets you will need to utilize in order to buy a house. In the Assets section, it's fine to draw from cash accounts, but leave the emergency fund and cash buffer in your primary checking account intact. If you need to tap tax-deferred retirement accounts such as an IRA or 401(k) to meet the up-front costs of buying a house, then you are definitely better off waiting to buy a home.

These four questions overlook the emotional considerations in buying a home, but my goal is to help you make the best financial decision for long-term success. I understand the frustration of paying rent every month and feeling like you are throwing money away. But buying a home is not always the answer. Payments on a typical 15-year or 30-year mortgage mostly go toward interest costs in the early years and the upfront costs of a purchase are significant, too. If you plan to own your home for less than five years, then lower your expectations of building equity and understand that home ownership may have a negative impact on your net worth.

You've Decided to Buy. Now What?

Throughout the home-buying process, there is a lot of pressure to spend more than what makes sense for you. To avoid overextending yourself,

FIGURE **10.2**   ESTIMATING THE HOME PRICE YOU CAN AFFORD

	ESTIMATED MONTHLY EXPENSE
Gross Monthly Income × 25%	$_____
Total Monthly Debt Service (Principal + Interest)	$(_____)
Mortgage Payment You Can Afford	$_____
Mortgage Payment You Can Afford × 12 Months	$_____
÷ Mortgage Interest Rate Available	÷ _____%
× (1+ % Down Payment)	×_____
Home Price You Can Afford	$_____

review Figure 10.2 to calculate how much home you can afford. There are four key variables in this calculation:

1. Start with the percentage of gross monthly income you can dedicate to a monthly home payment, which I generally prefer to cap at 25 percent of gross monthly income. For metropolitan areas where real estate prices are higher than the rest of the country, a case can be made to boost that percentage to 36 percent.
2. Subtract out the total amount of monthly principal and interest payments for other debts such as a student or auto loans. Conventional lenders typically will not lend to people with total monthly debt service payments greater than 36 percent of gross monthly income. The less debt you have, the bigger the mortgage payment you can obtain.
3. The mortgage interest rate makes a dramatic difference in your purchasing power. The lower the interest rate on a mortgage, the more expensive a home you will be able to afford.
4. Your down payment also figures into the purchase price. The bigger the down payment, the more expensive a home you can afford.

To see how this works, let's compare two hypothetical homebuyers, Amy and Anthony (see Figure 10.3). Amy lives in San Francisco where real estate prices are higher than the rest of the country, so she is going to dedicate 36 percent of her gross monthly income to a mortgage payment. Amy earns $150,000 and currently spends $1,250 a month on principal and interest payments for a student loan. She plans to make a 20 percent

FIGURE **10.3**   ESTIMATING THE HOME PRICE AMY AND ANTHONY CAN AFFORD

	AMY	ANTHONY
Gross Monthly Income × (36% for Amy and 25% for Anthony)	$4,500	$3,125
Total Monthly Debt Service (Principal + Interest)	($1,250)	($250)
Mortgage Payment They Can Afford	**$3,250**	**$2,875**
Mortgage Payment You Can Afford × 12 Months	$39,000	$34,500
÷ Mortgage Interest Rate Available	÷4%	÷4%
× (1+% Down Payment)	× 1.20	× 1.25
Home Price They Can Afford	**$1,170,000**	**$1,078,125**

down payment and can obtain a mortgage interest rate of 4 percent. Given Amy's inputs, she is able to afford a house that costs $1,170,000.

Meanwhile, Anthony also earns $150,000 but lives in St. Louis, where real estate prices are lower. As a result, he is going to dedicate only 25 percent of his gross income to a mortgage payment. Anthony pays $250 a month in principal and interest toward an auto loan. He has been saving for a down payment on a house for a long time, so he is planning to put 25 percent down and will obtain a mortgage with a 4 percent interest rate. Given Anthony's inputs, he is able to afford a house that costs $1,078,125.

Just because you can spend a certain amount on a house doesn't mean you should. Keep this in mind as you decide where to cap the amount of monthly income you dedicate to a mortgage payment. In my experience, 25 percent of gross monthly income is prudent. A few reasons that may justify a higher percentage include having a high degree of certainty about earning more income in the future, planning to live in the house for at least 10 years, or living in an area where real estate prices are relatively stable.

As for your down payment, the best practice is to put down 20 percent of the purchase price. One argument for making a bigger down payment is it creates a smaller loan and less interest costs over time. However, a larger down payment is rarely a better choice than building up an emergency fund or contributing to your investment portfolio.

For people putting less than 20 percent down, I generally recommend they continue renting, but it's possible to obtain a conventional mortgage with the help of private mortgage insurance (PMI). Lenders require PMI because borrowers are more likely to default on a loan in which they have very little invested. While paying for PMI increases the cost of owner-ship, the payments aren't permanent. Once you have built up 20 percent equity in your home, PMI payments go away and leave you with just the mortgage payment.

Common Mistakes People Make When Buying a Home

The biggest mistake people make when purchasing a home is not living there long enough for the finances to work out in their favor. If you are on the fence about staying in the same home at least five years, then you should favor renting. Other common mistakes we've discussed are under-estimating the cost of homeownership and buying more home than you can afford. Completing the **Rent versus Buy Worksheet** and the **Buying a Home Worksheet** on **peterlazaroff.com/worksheets** will help protect you from falling victim to these mistakes.

Another mistake is viewing your home purchase as an investment rather than a place to live. Unlike professional real estate investors, most of our real estate success will boil down to good timing and luck. Unlike a traditional portfolio of stocks and bonds, a home is an illiquid and indivisible asset—you can't slice off a piece of your kitchen and sell it for cash. Owning a home is also an extremely undiversified bet on a single neighborhood in a single geographic region. Homes also offer very little long-term price appreciation after adjusting for inflation. According to historical data from Nobel Laureate Robert Shiller, home prices have risen only 0.37 percent per year after adjusting for inflation over the past 125 years.[6] Not only are the price gains minimal, but you must spend additional capital on maintenance and improvements to prevent your home value from depreciating over time—not exactly something you want to see in an investment.

A common mistake that occurs in the actual buying process includes forgoing expert advice during the process. The assistance of an agent or broker can be especially helpful to a first-time homebuyer, but even people buying their second or third homes should enlist the help of a professional. Just be sure to find out how he or she is being compensated so that you understand their motivations throughout the purchasing process. In addi-tion, paying for a detailed inspection acts as insurance against getting sold a lemon. It can save you tens of thousands of dollars and months of time.

---

[6]www.econ.yale.edu/~shiller/data.htm.

CHAPTER ELEVEN

Big Financial Decisions at Critical Junctions in Life

When major financial decisions come only once or twice in a life-time, it's important to get to them right. Those pivotal moments certainly include some of the things we discussed in the previous chapter such as starting a family or buying a home. Now our focus shifts to some additional major life decision points that impact you and your family's well-being. Let's walk through these important decisions you'll likely need to make at some point, so you can understand how to get it right the first time.

WHY YOU NEED AN ESTATE PLAN (NO, THEY'RE NOT "JUST FOR REALLY RICH PEOPLE")

Developing and executing an estate plan is one of the most important pieces of anyone's financial plan. No, estate plans are not just for really rich people—you need one to protect yourself, your family, and your assets. Estate planning is a process designed to manage and preserve your assets during your lifetime. Estate plans also conserve and control the distribution of your assets after your death in a way that aligns with your goals and objectives. It starts with the following five documents everyone needs, regardless of age, health, or level of wealth.

1. **Will**

    At the crux of any estate plan, a will indicates how you want your property distributed after your death. Without a will, disbursements are made according to state law—and those laws might not align with your priorities. A will also names an executor to manage and settle your estate as well as a legal guardian for any dependents. Since this is a legal document, it is crucial that a will is well written so that it is properly executed under your state's laws.

2. **Letter of Instruction**

    A letter of instruction is a nonlegal document that may accompany your will to express personal thoughts and directions. Unlike a will, the letter of instruction remains private and its directions are not binding.

3. **Durable Power of Attorney**

    A durable power of attorney (DPOA) authorizes someone to act on your behalf should you become physically or mentally unable to handle financial matters. The person you designate in the DPOA can pay bills, file taxes, direct investments, and complete important money management tasks on your behalf.

4. **Advanced Medical Directives**

    Advanced medical directives allow you to specify the medical treatments you desire in the event you can't express that on your own. These directives also appoint someone to make medical decisions if you are incapacitated. Without this document, medical care providers must prolong your life using artificial means if necessary. The three types of advanced medical directives are a living will, a durable power of attorney for health care, and a Do Not Resuscitate order.

5. **Living Trust**

    A living trust, also known as a revocable or inter vivos trust, creates a separate legal entity to own property. Your assets will avoid going through probate if you put a living trust into place. Probate is well worth avoiding because it can be costly and time consuming—not to mention emotionally taxing—for your friends, family, and heirs.

    Probate can also interfere with the management of a closely held business or stock portfolio. As you can see in Figure 11.1, your estate becomes public record by going through probate, but having a trust in place generally prevents public knowledge of your estate.

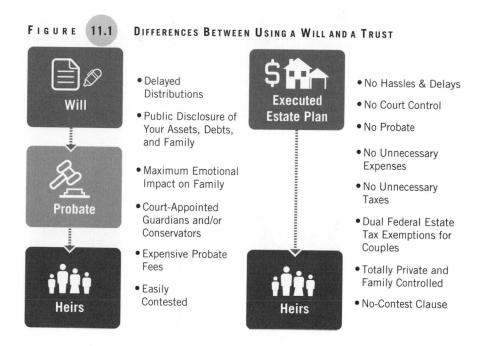

FIGURE 11.1   DIFFERENCES BETWEEN USING A WILL AND A TRUST

Will
- Delayed Distributions
- Public Disclosure of Your Assets, Debts, and Family

Probate
- Maximum Emotional Impact on Family
- Court-Appointed Guardians and/or Conservators
- Expensive Probate Fees
- Easily Contested

Heirs

Executed Estate Plan
- No Hassles & Delays
- No Court Control
- No Probate
- No Unnecessary Expenses
- No Unnecessary Taxes
- Dual Federal Estate Tax Exemptions for Couples
- Totally Private and Family Controlled
- No-Contest Clause

Heirs

Ask five different estate attorneys when it makes sense to get estate planning documents, and you might receive five different opinions. Here's my take: the trigger point for having a full set of estate planning documents is when you get married. Before getting married, you should get a durable power of attorney and an advanced medical directive if you want to have a say over medical and financial decisions should you become incapacitated. Prior to getting married, you would also need a will if you feel strongly about who should receive your money, property, and possessions in the event of your death.

What Happens After You Create an Estate Plan?

After executing your estate plan, make sure the executors and trustees are aware of your wishes and know where your documents are located. You want to keep the documents in a safe place, of course, but not so safe that they can't be found when needed. It's also helpful to create an estate memo listing all your financial information. Staying organized helps ease the burden of administering your estate for your loved ones.

Finally, it's important to review your estate plan every few years to make sure it remains up to date with current laws and reflects your wishes as your life changes. With my own clients, we perform an estate plan review every other year. If you don't have an advisor with estate planning experience, then reviewing it with an attorney every five years is reasonable. Other trigger points for an estate planning review include major life events like:

- Changes in your marital status
- Changes in the marital status of your children or grandchildren
- Additions to your family through birth, adoption, or marriage
- The death of a spouse or family member
- A family member becomes ill, dependent on you, or incapacitated
- A substantial change in the value of your assets or in your plans for their use
- Receiving a sizable inheritance or gift
- A change in the amount of income you make or need
- Retirement

Life typically gets more complex as you age and build wealth. This makes it crucial to implement an estate plan early and review it regularly. Estate planning is a little different for everyone. The process may seem overwhelming, but once you execute an estate plan, your peace of mind will be worth it.

Common Estate Planning Mistakes

The biggest mistake people make with estate planning—aside from not having their documents in place—is failing to fund the vehicles those documents created by retitling assets. The work isn't done once you sign your documents. Your attorney should provide guidance on how to retitle your assets appropriately. This may include titling assets in the name of your trust, adding a transfer on death (TOD) designation to your tangible and investment assets, or a payable on death (POD) designation on your savings and checking accounts. It may also include putting a beneficiary deed on your house. Retitling assets requires some legwork, but it is far less painful than going through the probate process.

Another huge mistake people make is balking at the cost of estate planning documents and trying to draft legal documents themselves through an online service like LegalZoom. LegalZoom asks a series of questions to generate documents that address a general understanding of the law, but

LegalZoom's disclaimer clearly states the information they provide "is not legal advice and is not guaranteed to be correct, complete or up-to-date." It is important to work with an attorney who specializes in estate planning and is licensed in your state. Every state has its own set of laws dictating the way estates pass from the deceased to beneficiaries. The specific language required to comply with your state's unique laws is nuanced, so working with a professional ensures that your wishes are carried out with minimal strain on your heirs.

UNDERSTANDING LIFE INSURANCE: WHAT IT IS, WHY YOU NEED IT, AND HOW MUCH YOU NEED

Planning for death can be uncomfortable to say the least, but just about everyone with a family needs life insurance. Life insurance is an agreement in which the insurer promises to pay a certain sum at your death to one or more beneficiaries of your choosing. In exchange, you (the insured) make premium payments to the insurance company.

The most common reason for buying life insurance is to replace the income lost if you were to pass away. Proceeds from a life insurance policy make cash available to support your family almost immediately. The payout could be used to repay any debt that you may leave behind (mortgages, car loans, student loans, and credit card balances) or estate taxes. Life insurance proceeds might also be used to fund a surviving spouse's retirement or college tuition costs for any of the deceased's children.

Your need for life insurance changes over time. When you are young, you typically have less need for a policy. As your family grows, protecting those who depend on you becomes increasingly important. As your children grow into adults who can earn money for themselves, your need for life insurance diminishes. By the time you are ready to retire, life insurance is no longer necessary.[1]

When (and How Much) Life Insurance Makes Sense

Whether or not you need life insurance can be addressed by one question: Do I have other people counting on me for my income? If your answer is "yes," then you probably need a policy.

Most people realize the potentially disastrous consequences of not insuring the primary earner, but a stay-at-home spouse also needs insurance because his or her death would require replacing costly childcare

---

[1] Possible exceptions to this are having children with special needs or a taxable estate.

and housekeeping expenses. For single-income families, both spouses need enough coverage to replace their partner's income or the economic value of lost services that would result from their death. For dual-income families, it's unlikely that the surviving spouse will be able to keep up with the household expenses, pay for childcare, and make sufficient retirement savings contributions with the remaining income. In most situations, both parents should carry coverage.

How much insurance you need depends on your marital status, family size, financial obligations, career stage, and goals for the policy. To better estimate how much life insurance you need, consider your responses to the following questions:

- What immediate financial expenses, like debt repayment or funeral costs, would your family face upon your death?
- How much of your salary goes to current expenses versus saving for future needs such as retirement?
- How long would your dependents need support if you died today?
- How much money would you want to leave for special situations, such as funding your children's education, gifts to charities, or leaving an inheritance for your children?

The answers to these questions help estimate an appropriate policy size. I'd also consider using an insurance calculator (e.g., www.bankrate.com/calculators and www.360financialliteracy.org/calculators) before engaging an insurance professional. Many of the life events that trigger an estate plan review are a good opportunity to reassess your insurance, but the best practice is to review your coverage needs annually.

What to Consider Before Buying Life Insurance

There are two basic types of life insurance: term and permanent. Term insurance provides coverage for a specific period of time, usually between one and 30 years. If you live to the end of the term, the policy terminates and you stop paying premiums. Some policies can be renewed annually at the end of the term with increasing premium payments until you reach age 95. Term insurance is the answer for almost everyone because you can get much more coverage (also called a death benefit) at a fraction of the cost of permanent insurance. That said, there are times when permanent insurance makes sense.

Permanent life insurance provides protection for your entire life as long as you continue paying the premium and the insurer remains solvent. Permanent life insurance comes in three broad flavors: whole life, universal life, and variable life. Premiums are greater than the cost of insurance in the earlier years so that a reserve, known as the cash value, can be accumulated to make up the shortfall in premiums necessary to insure you later. If the policy owner stops paying premiums and terminates the policy, the cash value is returned to the policy owner (subject to applicable surrender or early withdrawal charges). If your cash value exceeds the amount of premiums you've paid over the life of the policy, then the policy owner owes ordinary income taxes on the difference upon surrender.

Permanent policies are quite a bit more expensive, so there are only a few instances to consider this type of policy. People who have children with special needs are good candidates for a permanent policy, and this type of coverage might also make sense if you're likely to have a taxable estate.[2] Asset protection against creditors, divorce, or lawsuits is another potentially reasonable cause for buying permanent insurance over term, but a good estate plan is usually more cost effective for asset protection.

When it's time to buy a policy, an insurance broker can shop different providers for a policy that best fits your unique needs. You can also shop around online yourself and buy directly from an insurance company. Just know that any policy you buy is only as good as the company that issues it. You might find a dirt-cheap rate, but the company may not be as financially stable as a company charging slightly higher premiums. Rating services such as Moody's and Standard & Poor's can help you evaluate an insurer's financial strength, but these are not foolproof.

Another way to obtain insurance coverage is through a group life insurance plan from your employer or a professional association. While premiums through group life insurance plans are substantially cheaper than buying an individual policy, there are some downsides. If you ever leave your employer or the association, the policy may lapse and buying a new policy will require new medical exams. A new medical exam is problematic if you develop a health condition that results in higher premiums or being denied coverage altogether. You'll also be older and premiums increase with age.

In general, it's best to use a group plan to supplement a primary individual policy. The exception would be if you have a preexisting medical condition that prevents you from buying life insurance elsewhere. In this case, buy as much as you can through the group plan. Some employers offer an option to convert your group coverage to an individual policy if you leave the company. This will cost significantly more than the premium you were paying while employed, but it may be the only way to get insurance with a preexisting medical condition coverage.

---

[2] The 2019 federal estate and gift tax limit is $11,400,000 per person.

Common Mistakes People Make When Buying Life Insurance

Unfortunately, it's common to see people buy permanent insurance when term insurance is the better solution. To avoid purchasing the wrong policy, it helps to understand the conflicts of interest as well as commonly used sales tactics.

My first exposure to life insurance sales was a summer program where college interns obtained their license to sell life insurance. Because the company and agent made far more money selling permanent insurance, the sales training emphasized a series of one-liners to convince people to buy costlier permanent insurance instead of a cheaper term policy. The following are common one-liners I still hear today, followed by refuting information to help you avoid falling into this sales trap.

"Buy life insurance while you are young and healthy because rates are low."

As a young adult, your death would not create financial hardship for others, unless you're married or have children. For most young singles, life insurance is not a priority. Premiums are lower for young people who are healthy, which makes sense because their probability of dying is lower. However, paying insurance premiums when nobody is dependent on your income is a big mistake, especially if you could be putting that money toward other goals like retirement or buying a home. The difference in earnings you could realize by investing the money instead of paying permanent insurance premiums is enormous.

"Why rent a policy when you could own it?"

Insurance agents sometimes compare buying permanent insurance to building equity in a home, but this doesn't make any sense. The choice to rent or buy a home is completely different because you always need a place to live, whereas your need for life insurance disappears at the end of the term policy. More importantly, the cost of renting versus owning an insurance policy is drastically greater than the long-term difference in renting versus owning a home. Building equity in a home isn't the best way to accumulate wealth in the first place—building wealth inside a permanent insurance policy is worse. Investing the cost savings from buying a term policy versus a permanent policy is a far superior method for accumulating wealth. In addition, you can access your investments or savings without the restrictions that come with taking a loan on a permanent insurance policy. That brings me to the next one-liner.

"With the growing cash balance, you can be your own bank and take loans from the policy."

When the liquidity of a permanent life insurance policy comes into question, insurance salespeople point to the ability to take loans from the cash value. As the cash value of your policy grows—which, by the way, takes a very long time—you could take a loan against a certain percentage of the cash value. However, to maintain the death benefit and recover the lost effect of compounding on the funds being withdrawn, the policy charges a high interest rate on the amount withdrawn—plus, you must keep paying premiums.

If you fail to make premium or interest payments, the death benefit decreases and the policy eventually terminates. At that point, you'll owe ordinary income taxes on the loan amount and remaining cash value minus the amount of premiums paid during the life of the policy. A permanent policy is not the personal piggy bank that an insurance salesperson might suggest. It is a highly illiquid and costly way to accumulate savings.

"Permanent insurance is a form of forced savings."

This is a terrible reason to buy insurance. You buy insurance to protect your family against the loss of income and the value of your household contributions. A permanent insurance policy lacks the flexibility and liquidity necessary to live life on your own terms. The best form of forced savings is setting up an automated plan to fund your goals.

"Look at those dividends in the policy. You can't earn those in your portfolio. Plus, that growth is tax free!"

By law, an insurance salesperson can't refer to a whole life insurance policy as an "investment vehicle," and for good reason. Still, they lean heavily on the idea of "dividend growth" when presenting a policy illustration. Dividends for a permanent whole life insurance policy are a combination of the investment gains the insurer earns on your capital, plus the difference between how much the company collected in premiums versus how much they paid out in death benefits. Dividends are an estimate, but they are rarely emphasized as such. Policy illustrations often restate projected dividends and future cash value, so the projected growth of your cash value is far from guaranteed.

> *"You already have some of your savings going to your retirement accounts. You can think of your policy as a form of diversification."*

You hear this argument when agents pitch you almost any form of permanent insurance. With a variable or universal life policy, you might also hear something along the lines of "You can capture market upside, but protect against the downside." This is because part of your premium payments go to the purchase of insurance and the rest goes to a super expensive stock investment. The most cost-effective and flexible approach is buying term insurance to financially protect your loved ones and investing your savings in a low-cost portfolio for long-term growth.

PROTECT YOUR MOST IMPORTANT ASSET WITH DISABILITY INSURANCE

When my wife and I were expecting our first child, we were quick to get term life insurance policies in place. It wasn't until our first child was nearly five years old, however, that I protected my human capital from disability. I'm not alone, either. While most people see life insurance as a no-brainer to protect against losing their income due to death, few people consider protecting their human capital in the event they become sick or injured. But I'm actually far more likely to become disabled before retirement than I am to die—and so are you.

The Social Security Administration estimates that 91.2 percent of women and 85.6 percent of men will live to age 67. Meanwhile, the same report projects that a 20-year-old has a 26.8 percent chance of being disabled for at least 12 months before reaching retirement at age 67.[3] Once you become disabled, the Council for Disability Awareness reports that the average long-term disability absence lasts for 34.6 months— nearly three years! In other words, our chances of enduring a period of time in which we're disabled and unable to work is much more likely than the chances of us dying prior to retirement. And when you are in the early or middle stages of your career, there are few (if any) assets more valuable than your ability to earn an income.

[3]Johanna Maleh and Tiffany Bosley, "Disability and Death Probability Tables for Insured Workers Born in 1997," Social Security Administration Actuarial Note Number 2017.6, October 2017. Note that the definition of disabled in this report is far more strict than you would see in a group or individual policy.

Why Most People Don't Get Disability Insurance

When I thought about disability insurance earlier in my career, the scenarios that always came to mind involved losing a limb or going blind. Because my profession does not involve physical labor or operating heavy machinery, I assumed that such severe disabilities would only modestly impact my ability to earn an income. My incredibly ignorant mindset also overlooked the wide range of opportunities for becoming physically disabled, from a car accident to slipping on ice.

Behavioral economists would point out that I suffered from optimism bias, or the tendency to believe that bad things are more likely to happen to other people. When you hear statistics about negative life events, you naturally feel it is unlikely to happen to you. With this mindset, the price tag for disability insurance seems sky high—and no, it is not cheap, but we will deal with that in a moment.

The other problem with my previous mindset is that I was mostly thinking about disability in terms of physical injury. What I was not considering in delaying the purchase of a disability policy is that debilitating, but not always deadly, illnesses like cancer don't care about your age or occupation. While I was unlikely to be involved in some sort of forklift accident in my work as a financial advisor, I could have easily been diagnosed with a disease that prevented me from working.

In fact, I watched this very thing happen to a client after he was diagnosed with an illness that forced him to leave his job at an inopportune time. Without the disability policies he had purchased outside of his employer, his family would have experienced a dramatic reduction in lifestyle at best. At worst, and probably more likely, they wouldn't have been able to make ends meet. Being close to his experience motivated me to finally take action. I got my act together and got the proper disability coverage in place.

Considerations for Disability Insurance

If you're like me, it may take you awhile to land on a policy because of the high costs, myriad of options within different policies, or underlying optimism that you won't become disabled. Here are a few things that may help with your decision.

If you rely on a paycheck, you need to have disability coverage.

Your need is particularly pronounced if you are married or have children because others likely depend on your contribution to the household. The need for disability decreases once you accumulate enough retirement savings to make do if a disability forced you into early retirement. The need for disability insurance also decreases once your children or spouse no longer require your financial support.

Don't worry about buying a short-term policy.

You are much better off building up your emergency fund and self-insuring against a short-term disability. Not only is this approach cheaper, it provides greater flexibility and liquidity. Short-term disability policies vary, but they generally cover up to 180 days. Long-term disability insurance picks up where the short-term leaves off and covers you anywhere from a few years to the rest of your life. If you are buying disability insurance, seek out a long-term policy that pays benefits until age 65.

Figure out what you can afford and get a long-term policy within your budget.

Disability policies come in all shapes and sizes. When you work with a good, fee-only financial advisor, they can find highly customized coverage based on what you are able to afford. If you are still concerned about the cost, there are ways to get less expensive coverage. You may consider reducing the monthly benefit amount, shortening the benefit period (the amount of time you receive benefits if disabled), lengthening the elimination period (the amount of time you must be disabled before benefits are paid), eliminating cost-of-living adjustments, and so on.

Don't underestimate the amount of coverage you need.

Most people think about coverage in terms of their current spending trends, but your medical expenses can skyrocket if your disability forces you to quit your job and your group medical insurance coverage is terminated. You may also need to buy medical equipment or supplies, or in some extreme cases, renovate your home to accommodate a disability. Childcare expenses are also likely to rise if your children can't drive themselves. With young children, simply going from two sets of able hands to one might necessitate hiring help with the kids or other household chores like cooking, cleaning, laundry, and lawn maintenance.

Don't assume your employer–paid coverage is enough.

According to the Bureau of Labor Statistics, about one-third of employers offer a disability policy, but these plans replace only a small amount of income and lack the duration to protect against an extended absence from work. Employer plans typically offer short-term policies covering 60 to 70 percent of your salary with a $1,000/week cap for up to three months. In some cases, employers will offer access to group long-term disability insurance policy covering 50 to 70 percent of your salary with caps between $5,000 and $10,000 per month.[4] Most employers only use base salary, excluding commissions or bonuses, to calculate your disability benefits. Reviewing your **Cash Flow Worksheet** should make it clear whether your employer-paid coverage is sufficient.

Consider purchasing coverage through a group plan.

Purchasing coverage through a group plan is usually cheaper than buying an individual policy. Some employers allow you to purchase supplemental long-term insurance as an elective benefit. Similarly, some professional associations offer group disability coverage that is tailored to their profession. Although group plans make purchasing an individual policy substantially cheaper, remember that you lose coverage when you change jobs or leave the professional association.

Remember, Disability Is More Likely than Death

Aside from estate planning, disability insurance is the biggest gap in most people's financial plan. If you are comfortable buying life insurance, you should not balk at the idea of disability insurance. You are more likely to become disabled during your career than you are to die. Accidents can happen everywhere and illness can strike anyone. Don't leave a gaping hole in your own otherwise comprehensive financial picture. Use this as the prod you may need to stop procrastinating and start protecting your most important asset.

BUILDING A COMPREHENSIVE FINANCIAL PLAN

The content of this chapter is the densest and most complicated in this entire book. While many people can implement an efficient system for saving toward goals and investing those dollars in a disciplined manner, it is a far bigger task to sufficiently plan for an unexpected death or disability. Consequently, you may eventually find yourself needing to hire a financial professional. Before hiring a professional, you must understand the different types of advisors and how to identify the right one for you.

---

[4]If you pay policy premiums with after-tax dollars, the benefits you receive will be tax free. Premiums paid with pretax dollars, usually through your employer, may cause the benefits to be taxable when received.

CHAPTER TWELVE

How to Create Your Own Team of Professionals to Help You Succeed

Feeling overwhelmed from any of the in-depth explanations of how to get your financial house in order and keep it that way forever? Don't worry: that's a natural and normal feeling. Financial planning is more like an ongoing full-time job than a one-time task to tackle. Hiring a financial professional often makes implementing a comprehensive financial plan easier and more effective.

As a financial planner, I'm obviously biased, but allow me to share a quick story to give more context to my suggestion to hire help. When I bought my first home in May 2010, I was dead-set on having a big yard. With that bigger yard came bigger responsibilities. Devoting time and effort to maintaining the lawn required about 90 minutes a week, but I always felt the time commitment was manageable.

There were some occasions, however, when I didn't have time to cut the grass. Sometimes that was due to other commitments and, admittedly, sometimes it was just due to laziness. In an ideal world, fitting in 90 minutes for lawn care would be no problem. But in real life, things happen. Stuff comes up. Distractions abound. Other opportunities present themselves that sound better than doing chores.

Postponing my yardwork meant dealing with much longer grass when I did get around to mowing it. Longer grass meant it took more time to cut and the lawn didn't look as nice. It was even worse when I put it off a day without looking at the weather only to be surprised by three days of rain. Then cutting the grass really became a problem. But all and all, I got by just fine. My lawn looked pretty good and I didn't see a reason to do it any differently.

That all changed the summer I hired a guy named Leo to cut my grass for $35 a week so I could spend more time with my wife and newborn son. Leo did little things I wouldn't have thought about or known how to do properly. He periodically changed the direction in which he cut the grass to encourage healthier growth. He fertilized and seeded strategically. He cut the grass a specific length depending on weather conditions or an area's exposure to the sun. He edged around our flower beds and plants. The end result was a dramatically healthier and superior-looking lawn. Not only that, but hiring Leo created time for me to focus on more important things in life.

People who take a do-it-yourself approach to any job—be it landscaping or financial planning—do so to save money or because they enjoy the work. Do-it-yourselfers are also okay with "getting by just fine," as I was with my lawn, but the difference between "just fine" and doing well with your money is significant. Much like Leo did a variety of things to improve my lawn's health and appearance, a financial professional does things you would never think to do.

Building and executing a financial plan is not necessarily rocket science, but not knowing what you don't know can seriously limit success. Plus, mistakes can cost huge amounts of money. The mistakes and missed wealth-enhancing opportunities aren't always obvious to do-it-yourselfers because they don't possess the tools to accurately evaluate their financial decisions. Financial advisors, on the other hand, have the tools and processes to dramatically improve your financial outcomes. In fact, an ongoing Vanguard study estimates that financial advisors add "about 3 percent" in relative return to an individual's investments. Figure 12.1 outlines the best practices that contribute to Vanguard's estimate of a financial advisor's value.

As Vanguard's study explains, the value of an advisor is not consistent over time and you shouldn't expect that 3 percent to show up every year. There are times when fear or greed may tempt you to deviate from a thoughtfully crafted investment plan. In this instance, your advisor could add tens of percentage points by guiding you to stay the course and avoid losses—such valuable interventions can offset a lifetime of fees.

FIGURE 12.1 HOW VANGUARD APPROXIMATES THE INVESTMENT VALUE OF AN ADVISOR

ADVISOR ALPHA STRATEGY	POTENTIAL VALUE RELATIVE TO "AVERAGE" CLIENT EXPERIENCE
Portfolio Construction	
Suitable Asset Allocation Using Broadly Diversified Mutual Funds/ETFs	> 0.00%
Cost-Effective Implementation (Expense Ratios)	0.40%
Asset Location	0.00%–0.75%
Total Return vs. Income Investing	> 0.00%
Wealth Management	
Rebalancing	0.35%
Spending Strategy (Withdrawal Order)	0.00%–1.10%
Portfolio Construction	
Advisor Guidance	0.35%
Potential Value Added	**"About 3%"**

It's also worth pointing out that the study doesn't attempt to quantify the value of comprehensive financial planning because, as the authors noted, we don't need to see oxygen to know it's beneficial.

Who do you want performing medical procedures on you: the unflappable do-it-yourselfer or a properly trained surgeon? That answer is pretty obvious for most people. You would probably also turn to a lawyer to interpret laws or argue a case in court on your behalf. Surgeons and lawyers spend years receiving specialized education and their skills are enhanced throughout their career with regular practice. People are quick to hand over jobs to those professionals. There are also high barriers to carrying out medical or legal tasks on your own, but there are absolutely no barriers to investing on your own. Anyone can invest money on their own, but research shows us time and again that they are likely to do worse than if they hired a financial advisor.

While the Vanguard study is one of many that highlight the enhancements a professional can make to your portfolio, your decision to hire a professional shouldn't be only about investments. Choosing an advisor who provides comprehensive financial planning beyond traditional investment advice can get your entire financial house in order and keep it that way forever. This includes proactively assisting in retirement planning, estate planning, tax projections, insurance analysis, entitlement strategies, and more—just as importantly, a financial professional makes sure all these aspects work in harmony.

Perhaps most important of all, hiring a professional frees you up to do the things you love most in life and alleviates the stress that can come from managing your own financial matters.

NOT ALL FINANCIAL PLANNERS ARE CREATED EQUAL: WHAT MAKES A "REAL" FINANCIAL PLANNER

While I am biased in thinking that choosing a good advisor is one of the best decisions you can make, I'm not naïve to the fact that choosing the wrong advisor can do more harm than good. Choosing a financial advisor can be a confusing process, especially because different professionals adhere to different standards of client care. Making matters worse are the litany of fancy titles and the alphabet soup of designations that professionals stick on their business cards.

If you are going to hire a professional, the most important investment you can make is the time you put into selecting the right person. This starts by understanding some of the major differences between professionals in the industry. Even when two professionals go by the title "advisor," it does not mean they provide the same service or adhere to the same ethical standards.

Differences in Standards of Care

Most people don't realize that different financial professionals are held to different standards of care. The fiduciary standard requires that an advisor put a client's interest first. Registered Investment Advisors (RIAs) adhere to the fiduciary standard and they are regulated by the Securities and Exchange Commission (SEC), which enforces the rules around what it means to be a fiduciary.

The suitability standard does not require advice to be in the client's best interest. The suitability standard only requires a broker to make recommendations that are "suitable" based on a client's personal situation. This standard is enforced through self-regulatory organizations called the National Association of Securities Dealers (NASD) and the Financial Industry Regulatory Authority (FINRA). Brokers or registered representatives are held only to this suitability standard and not the fiduciary standard. While they may call themselves "advisors," they're salespeople with a vested interest in getting you to buy specific financial products.

Imagine you need a new car, but you don't know much about the different options available. You head to the closest car dealer, which happens to be a Ford dealership, and the dealer asks you to describe what kind of car you need. You begin to list features and attributes that are best described as a Toyota Highlander, but you can find some of what you mention in a Ford Explorer, too. Under a suitability standard, the Ford dealer could say, "A Ford Explorer sounds like a good fit and we have some of those right over here," and never mention that a Toyota Highlander more closely aligns with your needs. The dealer makes the sale and earns a commission. You have a car that is suitable for your needs, but it isn't necessarily what's best for you.

The Ford dealer has a clear conflict of interest in this situation. The dealer can sell only Fords and will lose the opportunity to earn a commission if the client buys a Toyota Highlander. Under the suitability standard, the dealer can recommend the Ford Explorer, even if that is not necessarily what is best for you. Without a great deal of knowledge about the auto market, you wouldn't know you settled for what was only suitable.

Now, let's compare that to what happens under a fiduciary standard. If the car dealer acted as a fiduciary, the salesperson would be obligated to say, "It sounds like you are describing a Toyota Highlander. We don't sell those. In order to get the car that best fits your needs, go down the street to Toyota and ask for a Highlander." The dealer might mention a similar Ford model, but they'd also disclose that the Ford was more expensive and not exactly what you need. In this scenario, you have more information about your options as well as the dealer's financial incentives before choosing a car.

This same thing happens in the financial world. Financial professionals working under the suitability standard can sell you certain investments or insurance products that compensate them over competing options that might be a better fit for you. It is also common for financial professionals to have multiple industry affiliations that let them act as a fiduciary in some cases and not others. This allows the advisor to be a fiduciary in developing a financial plan or investment allocation, but then act under the suitability standard when implementing the recommendations. Talk about confusing.

It's unfair to expect the average person to know when an advisor is or isn't acting as a fiduciary. Most people using a financial professional have a hard time conceiving that the recommendations being made aren't in their best interests. Attorneys and accountants are required to put the interest of their clients first. Medical professionals do not put their own interests before the patient's. Why should financial advice be any different?

Many financial advisors always act as a fiduciary; you just need to know how to find them. One way is to use a Registered Investment Advisor (RIA) that is required by law to act as a fiduciary at all times. For additional assurance, some RIAs go the extra mile to be certified by the Centre for Fiduciary Excellence (CEFEX), which independently verifies that firms are fulfilling their fiduciary duty to the highest standard. You can check to see if an advisory firm is CEFEX certified by visiting www.cefex.org/CertifiedAdvisors.

Finally, you should require your advisor to put their fiduciary commitment in writing, otherwise they cannot be held accountable. Most fiduciaries put their fiduciary commitment in the client agreement you sign at the beginning of a relationship. If not, then ask your advisor to sign a fiduciary pledge.[1]

The Meaning of Various Advisor Titles and Credentials

Another area of confusion for consumers is the wide range of job titles and professional designations that people use to convey their expertise. While a job title might have some relevance to a firm's internal hierarchy, you can start with the assumption that all job titles are a form of marketing.[2] There's no reason to worry about whether your advisor's title is Wealth Manager, Planning Associate, Financial Planner, Portfolio Manager, Financial Consultant, Financial Specialist, Director, Senior Vice President, President, Principal, Partner, and so on. The title doesn't matter in the context of trying to find the best financial advisor for you.

While it's a challenge to understand the services someone will provide based on a title, the hundreds of professional designations are perhaps even worse. It is very rare these days to meet a financial professional without some combination of letters after his or her name on a business card. The problem is that not all letter combinations require the same degree of expertise, knowledge, or training. There are three designations that are most meaningful in the financial advice industry. All three require extensive knowledge, continuing education, and adherence to a strict code of ethics. They are listed in alphabetical order here.

[1] The Committee for the Fiduciary Standard created a pledge that can be downloaded from www.fi360.com/main/pdf/fiduciaryoath_individual.pdf.
[2] U.S. Securities and Exchange Commission, "Making Sense of Financial Professional Titles," *SEC-NASAA Investor Bulletin,* Pub. no. 160, September 2013.

Certified Financial Planner™ (CFP®)

This designation is the most comprehensive designation with regard to financial planning. Certification requires a lengthy education requirement prior to passing a comprehensive exam. The curriculum covers general principles of financial planning, education planning, insurance planning, investment planning, tax planning, retirement planning, and estate planning. The CFP® board requires you have three years of professional experience related to the financial planning process or two years of Apprenticeship experience that meets additional requirements. You should be confident in a CFP® recognizing issues that may affect your financial plan in all stages of your life.

Certified Public Accountant (CPA)

The CPA designation is focused on taxes and accounting. Before sitting for the CPA exam, candidates are required to have 150 semester hours of relevant courses. The CPA exam covers auditing and attestation, financial accounting and reporting, regulation, and business environment concepts. The prerequisite coursework and exam prepares a CPA to assist in strategic decision making for individuals, businesses, and other organizations.

Chartered Financial Analyst (CFA)

Financial professionals often consider the CFA designation to be the most difficult to earn. CFA Candidates must pass three exams, which each require roughly 300 hours of study and have a pass rate of just 42 percent.[3] The graduate level curriculum focuses on topics including portfolio management, economics, financial analysis, quantitative methods, and corporate finance. Before using the designation, CFA candidates need four years of professional work experience in investment decision making.

Differences in Compensation

The way financial professionals are compensated can impact objectivity. Fee-only advisors are paid only by their clients, which creates an incentive structure with the fewest conflicts of interest. The most common fee-only advisor is paid a percentage fee based on the amount of assets being managed, with that percentage fee decreasing as the account size increases.

[3] www.cfainstitute.org/programs/cfaprogram/Documents/1963_current_candidate_exam_results.pdf.

Other fee-only advisors charge by the hour or set fixed retainer fees for financial planning services. Because a fee-only advisor's compensation is not tied to a specific product or strategy, they can objectively provide advice without being swayed by personal benefits. This makes it easier for fee-only advisors to adhere to a fiduciary standard.

At the complete opposite end of the spectrum, a commission-only advisor earns income on products sold to the customer such as insurance products and mutual funds. They also earn income from transactions made and accounts opened for customers. The more activity a customer has, the more a commission-only advisor earns. Remember, a commission-only advisor works for his or her company, not you. The recommendations they make are filled with conflicts.

One final subtle distinction to note is between fee-only and fee-based advisors. Fee-only advisors are desirable because they always act as fiduciaries and their compensation closely aligns their interests with a client's interests. Fee-based advisors earn some of their revenue from fees paid by their clients, but also earn commissions from selling certain mutual funds, insurance policies, or brokerage products. Fee-based advisors adhere to the suitability rules, which means their financial recommendations may not be in your best interest and those conflicts of interest are harder to uncover.

HOW TO CHOOSE AN ADVISOR

Now that you understand some of the basic differences among financial professionals, we can focus on the process of hiring the right person for you. Fortunately, the Internet has all of the meaningful information needed to narrow down your choices to two or three prospective advisors. Here's how to start your search.

1. **Make a list of firms or people you know that you would consider hiring.**

   You may not know if people on your list act as a fiduciary at all times or carry one of the three professional designations I described earlier (CFP®, CPA, or CFA). That's okay for now. Feel free to ask family, friends, professional colleagues, or another trusted source to expand your list of advisor prospects. If you aren't comfortable asking others for referrals, then visit www.letsmakeaplan.org, which allows you to search CFP® professionals by city, state, or zip code. From there, you can narrow the search by portfolio size, type of advice, language capabilities, and advisor compensation.

2. **Visit www.brokercheck.finra.org to check each prospective advisor's record for misconduct.**

If the prospective advisor is a Registered Investment Advisor who is bound by the fiduciary standard, you'll be redirected to the Securities and Exchange Commission (SEC) website where all records of disputes (if any) are listed. If there's any record of misconduct, remove that advisor from your prospect list. These websites also list any credentials the prospective advisor has earned such as a CFP®, CPA, or CFA. Anyone without at least one of these designations should be crossed off your list as well.

3. **Visit prospective advisors' websites.**

While this is a bit like judging a book by its cover, a website contains valuable information about a person's background and capabilities. You might consider viewing a firm's blog to see if they have content that is relevant to you. Not every article needs to be tailored to your needs, but a firm that hasn't written about things that are important to someone in your stage of life probably doesn't have a lot of experience providing advice to someone like you. You can also check out a prospective advisor's LinkedIn profile for additional information.

4. **Narrow down your list to finalists.**

Send two or three advisors an email requesting a discovery meeting. They will undoubtedly have questions about you, but your questions are going to be more important at this stage. Equally important is how you ask those questions. People tend to ask different prospective advisors different questions, which makes comparisons tricky. You also must contend with the human brain—specifically, our memories are worse than we realize and our decision making is often biased by unimportant factors. The way to combat these issues is to hold a structured interview.

Structured Interview

The structured interview process was made popular by Nobel Prize–winning psychologist Daniel Kahneman to help reduce the impact of bias on our decision making. However, the first time I saw it applied to hiring a financial advisor was in a column by Jason Zweig of the *Wall Street Journal*.[4]

[4] Jason Zweig, "The Special Trick to Find the Right Financial Advisor," *The Wall Street Journal*, September 11, 2017. http://jasonzweig.com/the-special-trick-to-find-the-right-financial-adviser/.

The following is a list of the questions for a structured interview along with some commentary to help you identify responses that are in your best interest. I've also included some follow-up questions you might want to ask. If you add one of these follow-up questions to your list, then make sure to give the other prospective advisors an opportunity to answer those questions as well. After this list of questions are instructions for how to conduct and score a structured interview. For your convenience, you can download a **Structured Interview Worksheet** from **peterlazaroff.com/ worksheets**.

1. **How do you get paid?**

    Ideally an advisor is paid by the client and only by the client. If the firm is receiving revenue from any other sources, then there is opportunity for a conflict of interest.

2. **Does your firm earn revenue from anyone other than me?**

    The answer you want to hear is "no." Fee-only firms that generate revenue paid directly only by clients have the fewest potential conflicts of interest.

    Good follow-up questions:
    - Do you earn fees for referring clients to specialists like estate attorneys or insurance agents?
    - Do you participate in sales contests or award programs creating incentives to favor particular vendors?

3. **What services do you provide? Would you consider charging a retainer or by the hour instead of a percentage fee based on my assets?**

    Advisors who won't consider a financial planning fee are probably more focused on investment advice. They likely consider financial planning advice as an afterthought, meaning it will be far from comprehensive.

4. **How are you personally (not the firm) paid?**

    There isn't a perfect answer here, but it may uncover an individual's incentives. A salaried employee has fewer conflicts of interest than someone who gets paid a percentage of the revenue their clients generate.

5. **Do you always act as a fiduciary, and will you state that in writing?**

    Obviously, you want a clear and simple "yes" to this question. If the advisor isn't willing to put it in writing, then they can't be held accountable.

6. **Do you have experience working with clients like me?**

You want to work with someone who has experience dealing with issues that are relevant to you. If their response leaves you uncertain, you might consider asking what are the most common services clients like you receive.

7. **What experience, education, and credentials do you have?**

You should want someone with at least the Certified Financial Planner™ (CFP®) designation, but it's nice to also see someone who is a Chartered Financial Analyst (CFA) or Certified Public Accountant (CPA).

Good follow-up questions:
- Who else will I be working with, and what are their credentials?
- Is there a succession plan in place? If so, how far along into it are you? When do you anticipate the succession to be completed?

8. **What is your investment philosophy?**

Ideally, you want someone who believes in setting a long-term asset allocation and broadly diversifying using low-cost options. For firms that have multiple advisors, it's also important that they all follow the same investment strategy. When advisors don't share the same investment philosophy, it signals that your advisor may not have the time or resources to do proper due diligence on investments.

Good follow-up questions:
- What was the last change made to your firm's portfolios? Why was the change made?
- How often do you trade?
- How is my portfolio managed?
- What's your favorite investment in your own portfolio?
- Who manages your money?
- Do you believe you can beat the market?

9. **What is the all-in cost of working with you?**

Costs will vary depending on the size of your investment account and the financial planning services you require. The bigger your account, the smaller percentage fee you should expect, but there's no reason to pay more than 1 percent of the assets under management. Ideally an advisor's fee would cover all your financial planning needs.

10. **What is your overall impression of the advisor?**

This final question is for you to answer at the end of the interview before walking out of the room and should capture your gut feeling about an advisor. Try not to overthink it. This time you will score on a scale of one to five, with five being the best score. The purpose of this question is to capture the intangibles the other questions lack. Did the person communicate with too much jargon? Can you envision your kids one day working with this person? Do you feel comfortable sharing every detail of your financial life with this person?

If you have a significant other, you should both print the questions to individually and independently score the advisor's answers. You will want to rate each response on a scale of one to five immediately after you receive a response to your question. Don't look at each other's scores.

A structured interview is beneficial in a few ways. First, scoring all the questions on the same scale prevents one answer from coloring your judgment about other aspects of the advisor.[5] Second, the structured interview process prevents your brain from forming false memories by keeping an accurate measure of how you felt about an advisor's response. There will likely be some time lag between your different advisor interviews. Most people schedule advisor interviews over the course of a few weeks, but it could take longer if you have a busy schedule.

After you complete all your advisor interviews, add up the total scores for each score sheet. If you and your significant other scored the same advisor highest, go with that advisor. If there is a discrepancy, talk it out or find a way to reach a clear consensus. For example, you could ask your two favorite advisors to draft a sample financial plan for you to review and compare. They'll require you share personal information such as investment statements and tax returns, but this ought to help you identify the person who will best meet your needs.

This probably sounds like a lot of work, but it's a huge decision. As I expressed earlier, hiring a financial advisor can be the best decision you ever make—so long as you hire a good advisor. Following the process laid out here increases your chances of avoiding a bad advisor. Make sure to work through this process with your significant other, even if one person handles most of the household's finances. Alternatively, if you're single, you might consider bringing along a trusted friend or family member to provide a second set of scores.

---

[5] This is referred to as the halo effect.

USING A ROBO ADVISOR

"Robo advisor" is the industry term for a digital platform that automates your investments for a percentage fee based on your assets under management (see Figure 12.2). This growing segment serves a huge segment of investors who were previously forced to do it themselves, which opens most people up for a plethora of mistakes, or work with brokers who weren't required to act as fiduciaries.

Hybrid advisors go beyond automated investment portfolios by also providing financial planning through a digital platform you can use to track progress, make adjustments, and manage various goals. On top of the digital experience, hybrid advisors also provide you with access to Certified Financial Planner™ (CFP®) professionals to help further hone and personalize your financial plan.

Robo or hybrid advisors are the most cost-effective way for people with less than $500,000 in investable assets to manage their money. Nearly all digital advisors believe in the investment tenets expressed throughout this book, including long-term asset allocation, diversification, low costs, dollar

F I G U R E **12.2** ROBO VERSUS HYBRID VERSUS TRADITIONAL ADVISORS

ROBO ADVISORS	HYBRID ADVISORS	TRADITIONAL ADVISORS
Automated investment portfolio.	Automated investment portfolio based on your custom financial plan.	Professionally managed investment portfolio as part of your comprehensive financial plan.
No human advice or guidance.	Some human advice and at least annual guidance from a financial professional.	Proactive human advice and frequent meeting with a financial professional.
Low-cost, well-diversified portfolios.	Low-cost, well-diversified portfolios.	Low-cost, well-diversified portfolios.
Automatic rebalancing, dollar cost averaging, and tax-loss harvesting.	Automatic rebalancing, dollar cost averaging, and tax-loss harvesting.	Automatic rebalancing, dollar cost averaging, tax-loss harvesting, asset location, and tax-optimized savings/withdrawal strategies.
Lowest cost for least personalization and no financial planning.	Moderate cost for personalized advice and basic financial planning.	Highest cost for personalized advice, frequent meetings, and advanced financial planning techniques.

cost averaging, rebalancing, and tax-efficient portfolio strategies. If you also need financial planning, hybrid advisors provide financial planning advice at a fraction of the cost of a human financial planner.

In my opinion, there are two things to look for in a digital advisor: (1) being able to meet with a Certified Financial Planner™ (CFP®) at no additional cost because life is more complicated than an algorithm; and (2) a digital advisor that always acts as a fiduciary. Several digital advisors are Registered Investment Advisors (RIA), which means that by law they must always act in your best interest, but you can also look for the certified fiduciary designation from the Centre For Fiduciary Excellence (CEFEX). All CEFEX certified firms are listed at www.cefex.org/CertifiedAdvisors.

WHO ELSE DO YOU NEED ON YOUR TEAM?

If you are working with a financial advisor who provides comprehensive financial planning, he or she will help you build out your team of professionals. Whether you decide to do it yourself or use a digital advisor, you'll need to engage an estate attorney, accountant (digital or human), insurance broker, and banker. If you are doing it alone, the life events that necessitate working with these types of professionals don't occur often, but they are usually high-stakes situations that make it worth paying for help rather than doing it yourself.

Conclusion: Building a System for Financial Success

Financial success is not magic. After having read this book, it is my hope that you understand and believe that statement. The key to financial success is mostly about minimizing mistakes and leveraging the power of compounding across your entire financial life. The easiest way to do this is to define your goals, develop an optimal savings plan, and automate as much of your financial plan as possible.

Successful execution requires a systematic approach: one that helps you define your goals and create a road map to reach them. Your system should leverage the power of compounding by using an investment approach that focuses on low costs and asset allocation rather than picking the best investments and investing at the perfect time. Most importantly, your system must include behavioral buffers that help you keep your charted course—even when those tempting sirens do their best to lure you away or distract you from your tasks at hand.

The earlier you start, the easier reaching your goals will be. If you haven't started yet, let this book be your guide to making money simple. The information you now have makes you far more financially savvy than the average person, but that doesn't matter if you don't put that knowledge into action.

PUTTING INFORMATION AND MOTIVATION TO WORK WITH ACTIONABLE SYSTEMS

Knowledge is usually not enough to get people to change their behavior or pick up new habits. If dealing with your finances or even thinking about money is new to you, knowing what you should be thinking doesn't necessarily get you all the way to understanding how to apply that knowledge. In addition to motivation and information, you will likely need a few other tools to help you go from where you are today to where you would like to be in the future.

Most importantly, you need a system to keep you organized and on the right track. You need a way of taking action to work that system. That's why in addition to this book that can serve as your guide to all the knowledge and information you need, I put together a number of helpful worksheets to serve as the foundation of a system that gets you from knowing what to do—to actually taking the actions that will lead you to financial success.

WORKSHEETS AND STEP-BY-STEP INSTRUCTIONS TO ACHIEVING FINANCIAL SUCCESS

Using the worksheets described throughout the book will give you the direction you need. Taking the next step and automating your finances at every opportunity will help you resist the temptations that derail your progress toward your goals. Best of all, you can complete each worksheet in less than 30 minutes and reap the benefits for decades into the future.

What follows is a summary of the worksheets and steps you should take to get on track to making good decisions and protecting the lifestyle you currently enjoy.

❑ Download and complete the worksheets described throughout this book.
❑ Build a reverse budget and automate your finances.
❑ Leverage technology to save and invest for your goals.
❑ Protect yourself and your family with appropriate estate planning and insurance coverages.

That's just four steps! This system is designed to be simple. You don't need to overcomplicate your journey to financial success, particularly when you already have a mountain of responsibilities. High-pressure jobs, family obligations, managing the day-to-day errands and chores required to be a normally functioning adult, trying to maintain a social life, and hobbies outside of work—they all add up.

It's okay to feel overwhelmed by your finances, but it's not okay to let that stop you from making progress with your finances, because you don't have to do this alone. Using a financial professional can help you make smart choices about money so that you achieve your goals and fulfill your values dreams. Even better, a financial professional frees up valuable time for you to spend elsewhere.

If you're not sure whether using an advisor is right for you, take a look at my **Financial Wellness Assessment**. By visiting **smartmoneyquiz.com**, you can take a short quiz that identifies the strengths and weaknesses of your current financial situation. After completing the assessment, you will receive metrics on your financial wellness as well as recommendations and activities on what to do next.

ADDITIONAL RESOURCES

If you'd like to deepen your knowledge of personal finance or investing, here are some books I recommend to clients, friends, and family on a regular basis.

For Those Just Getting Started

The Elements of Investing: Easy Lessons for Every Investor by Burton Malkiel and Charles Ellis

The Little Book of Common Sense Investing: The Only Way to Guarantee Your Fair Share of Stock Market Returns by Jack Bogle

Happy Money: The Science of Happier Spending by Elizabeth Dunn and Michael Norton

30-Minute Money Solutions: A Step-By-Step Guide to Managing Your Finances by Christine Benz

For Those Looking to Advance Beyond the Basics

Winning the Loser's Game: Timeless Strategies for Successful Investing by Charles Ellis

A Random Walk Down Wall Street: The Time-Tested Strategy for Successful Investing by Burton Malkiel

The Four Pillars of Investing: Lessons for Building a Winning Portfolio by William Bernstein

A Wealth of Common Sense: Why Simplicity Trumps Complexity in Any Investment Plan by Ben Carlson
The Behavioral Investor by Daniel Crosby
All About Asset Allocation by Rick Ferri
Your Money and Your Brain: How the New Science of Neuroeconomics Can Help Make You Rich by Jason Zweig

For Those Interested in Taking a Deep Dive into More Complex Issues

Thinking, Fast and Slow by Daniel Kahneman
The Success Equation: Untangling Skill and Luck in Business, Sports, and Investing by Michael Mauboussin
Against the Gods: The Remarkable Story of Risk by Peter Bernstein
Fooled by Randomness: The Hidden Role of Chance in Life and in Markets by Nassim Taleb
The Most Important Thing Illuminated: Uncommon Sense for the Thoughtful Investor by Howard Marks

YOUR FREE SUBSCRIPTION TO BRIGHTPLAN

A good financial advisor can implement the systems and processes described in this book, but not everyone has enough money to access firms like Plancorp. That's a big reason why I decided to help build a single platform that implements a system to help people reach their financial goals. BrightPlan is a digital advisor that helps you set goals and calculate the necessary savings to reach them by your desired completion date. Then BrightPlan allows you to automate this financial plan by directing savings to each specific goal. Now you can view, adjust, and manage your financial plan from a single source rather than logging in to multiple applications. If you open an investment account with at least $500, you also can meet with a financial professional to ask questions and review your plan at no additional cost.

If you want to test out BrightPlan yourself, then visit **www.brightplan .com/simple** to receive a free three-month trial.

About the Author

Peter Lazaroff, CFA, CFP® is the Chief Investment Officer at Plancorp, a multi-billion-dollar wealth management firm serving individuals, institutions, and retirement plans across the country. Peter also serves as the Chief Investment Officer for BrightPlan, a digital advisor that builds customized financial plans and goals-based investment portfolios.

Peter plays a key role in developing and communicating his firms' investment strategy while also regularly contributing to the *Wall Street Journal* and *Forbes*. Peter also appears regularly on TV and in print media outlets such as *CNBC*, the *Wall Street Journal*, the *New York Times*, the *Financial Times, U.S. News, Barron's, MarketWatch*, and *Forbes*.

You can learn more about Peter by visiting **peterlazaroff.com**.

Quiz: Is Your Financial House in Order?

I want to help you make smart decisions with your money so that you can achieve all of your life goals. One way to speed up that process is by taking my Financial Wellness Assessment, which provides you with immediate feedback on your current situation and gives you next steps to get your entire financial house in order and keep it that way forever. Visit **smartmoneyquiz.com** to take the quiz.

Index